Mutual Funds Exposed
2nd edition

Mutual Funds Exposed
2nd edition

What You Don't Know May Be
Hazardous to Your Wealth

Kenneth A. Kim, PhD
Chief Financial Strategist,
EQIS Capital Management, Inc.

William R. Nelson, PhD
Chief Investment Officer,
EQIS Capital Management, Inc.

The statements and opinions discussed in this book are the opinions of the authors based on their 39 combined years of experience in academia. The discussions and opinions are intended solely for informational purposes. The stock symbols, company names, or other indicia discussed in the book are intended as examples only. Any such indicia used in a table or other calculation is purely hypothetical and not intended as an actual symbol or company name. Should any such indicia, now or in the future, be associated with an actual company, stock, or security, such association is purely coincidental.

Nothing in the book should be deemed a discussion of a specific investment company or product. Instead it is an academic narrative intended to discuss the mechanics of mutual funds and should not be construed as promoting a specific product or service. The book provides general non-investment specific commentary that invites the reader to learn more about the investment vehicles the reader may own.

Dr. Kenneth Kim and Dr. William Nelson are Investment Adviser Representatives of EQIS Capital Management, Inc. ("EQIS"), a registered investment adviser registered with the U.S. Securities and Exchange Commission. This is not an offer to sell securities or provide investment advice by either the authors or EQIS. Such advice may only be provided after a client suitability review is conducted and appropriate disclosures are made. Certain investment strategies may carry higher degrees of risk and have a level of complexity, which may not be suitable for all investors. Diversification does not ensure a profit or protect against loss in declining markets. All investments carry with them a degree of risk to include a total loss of principal. Past performance is not a guarantee of future results. Before investing you should identify, with the assistance of your financial adviser, your specific goals, risk tolerance, and investment time horizon.

EQIS Capital Management, Inc.
1000 4th Street, Suite 650
San Rafael, CA 94901
www.EQIS.com

First Printing, 2014
ISBN 978-0-9908249-0-9
Library of Congress Control Number: 2014917565

Second Printing, 2016
ISBN 978-0-9908249-1-6
Library of Congress Control Number: 2016903659

Printed in the United States of America

We dedicate this book to our children.
We save diligently and we invest wisely for you.

Table of Contents

Acknowledgements

Gracias, xie xie, merci, todah, gamsahamnida, shukran, danke, and thanks!

Many thanks to Terry O'Reilly, Andrew Leeah, and John Pollock, among others, who offered insightful and thoughtful comments on the first edition of *Mutual Funds Exposed*. We tried our best to incorporate their suggestions in this edition.

Foreword—from the first edition of *Mutual Funds Exposed*

It gives me great pleasure to write the foreword to this important (and entertaining) book. The author, Ken Kim, is my good friend, and I have greatly benefited from picking his brain about investments for the past twenty years. But, more importantly, Dr. Kim is a world-renowned expert in finance. In fact, I've had the pleasure to collaborate with him on a finance trade book, a college textbook, and numerous scholarly finance articles. So I know that Ken is always passionate about exposing the inefficiencies and myths of financial markets and the financial industry. I am not surprised that he wrote this book. It needed to be done, and he is just the person to do it! I am really glad that he did, and you will be too.

Everyone holds mutual funds. We own them directly, through brokerage accounts, and in our defined contribution plans. Mutual funds have always had their flaws, but for many decades, they were often the best investment vehicle that we had. But today, this is no longer the case. The investment industry has evolved to produce better ways to invest. Why are mutual funds obsolete and flawed investments? There are many reasons, and Ken has done a fantastic job at illustrating and explaining them in an entertaining and easy-to-understand style. Specifically, you may be shocked to learn about hidden costs, unfair taxes, and unproductive diversification. Read this book! Then evolve your portfolio to secure your finances for the future.

—Dr. John Nofsinger, PhD, author of the popular book, *Investment Madness*, the industry staple, *The Psychology of Investing*, 5th ed., and the college textbook, *Investments: Analysis and Behavior*

Preface

Remember when the only way we could call someone was with a phone that was on our desk or attached to a wall in our home or office? Remember when we looked up words in a thick dictionary, listened to cassette tapes, wrote papers on typewriters, composed letters to friends using pen and paper that took days to be delivered, got airline tickets sent to us in the mail? Remember when we drove around in new places with folded maps on our laps? There was even a time when we didn't know what a computer was. Today, we have smartphones, the Internet, emails/texts, GPSs, tablets, and so on. Because of technology, what we did in the past seems so funny and inefficient to us today.

I remember when we used to invest in mutual funds, but now we can have our very own separately managed accounts. It's funny to think about those old days. I still can't believe... ummm ... what? You don't know what I am talking about? Uh-oh, it looks like a part of you is still living in the past. If you are still primarily invested in mutual funds, then you are behind the times, and I think you should read this book. And I encourage you to do it now.

Mutual funds suffer from many flaws. Many of these flaws impose costs that are not always disclosed to you, including tax inefficiency (see chapter 2), high "hidden" costs (see chapter 3), and high management costs (see chapter 4). Mutual funds typically underperform relative to their benchmarks (see chapter 4), suffer from over-diversification (see chapter 5), are nontransparent (see chapter 6), and sadly, they may even be sneaky (see chapter 7).

But fear not. There is a modern alternative—your very own separately managed account (SMA) (see chapter 9) using multiple institutional money managers who can give you broad diversification and tax efficiency. This is how financial institutions, universities, and the super wealthy invest. And now, you can invest this way too. My goal in writing this book is to help you learn about this way of investing and to help you secure your financial dreams.

Welcome to the twenty-first century way of investing.

Note to the Reader

This book was written and researched by both authors but is in the voice of Dr. Kenneth A. Kim.

1 | Mutual Fund Challenges

The bad news—mutual funds are often a flawed and outdated way to invest.[1] Sorry about that; I guess I should have told you that I have both good news and bad news, and I should have asked you which you wanted to hear first. But don't worry, I'll get to the good news later. But first, the bad news—mutual funds, as investments, have challenges.

Perhaps the two most common reasons given for why mutual funds are bad investments are their opaque and high fees (i.e., you get charged a lot, but you have no idea

1

what those charges are) and their underperformance relative to benchmarks, such as the S&P 500 Index. There's actually much, much more to it than this. In fact, especially with today's technology, investing in mutual funds is, in my opinion, usually an archaic, costly, and inappropriate way to invest.

Many of the problems with mutual funds stem from the fact that the mutual fund owns the stocks and bonds in the mutual fund and that you as an investor can really only purchase "a claim" on the shares the fund owns, but you do *not* literally own any stocks or bonds in the fund. Instead, the mutual fund owns the stocks and bonds for you, and it also owns them for the many other people who buy the same mutual fund before you and after you. That is, your investment is "commingled" with other investors. In my opinion, this is a weird arrangement. For example, let's say you buy a mutual fund today, and your fund owns Google stock, which is priced at, let's say, five hundred dollars per share. Believe it or not, it does not count as though you bought Google stock at this price today because you literally did *not* buy Google stock today. Instead, you bought shares in a mutual fund today that bought Google stock a while ago. This is confusing, right? Well, maybe the mutual fund industry likes it when you're confused if confusion helps them get you to invest in their funds.

So, why is it so bad to be a commingled investor in a mutual fund? It can actually be a big problem for you. It can lead to tax inefficiency, high "hidden" costs, underperformance, and over-diversification. Other problems with mutual funds include non-transparency (i.e., most of the time, you cannot know what's in the fund, believe it or not) and sneaky behavior. I'll explain it all to you, in an easy-to-understand way. We'll start with what many consider to be one of the biggest flaws of mutual funds: their tax inefficiency.

Chapter 1 Notes

1. Mutual funds as outdated or flawed investments is
    written about frequently. For example, see:

    —Fabian, D. (2009, February 15). Mutual funds are hazardous to your
    wealth. *Market Watch*. Retrieved from http://www.marketwatch.
    com/story/investors-mutual-funds-hazardous-your-wealth

    —Guillot, C. (2013, March 11). Will mutual funds become
    obsolete? Retrieved from http://blog.betterinvesting/
    investing/will-mutual-funds-become-obsolete

    —Harris, B. (2013, June 20). The 10 biggest mutual funds:
    Are they really worth your money? *Forbes*. Retrieved from
    http://www.forbes.com/sites/billharris/2012/08/08/the-10-
    biggest-mutual-funds-are-they-really-worth-your-money

2 | Mutual Fund Tax Inefficiency

One reason why many experts say that buying mutual funds is a flawed way to invest is because of their tax inefficiency. Some people refer to this inefficiency as the embcddcd capital gains problem.[1] Here's a simple numerical example that helps illustrate the problem.

Let's say that you buy a mutual fund today, and it has ABC stock in it that is priced at $90 per share today. Later in the week, let's say that ABC's stock price drops to $80/share (ouch, that's too bad for you), and the fund then decides to sell the stock. Now, get ready to be surprised. Let's say that the fund had bought ABC stock at $75/share. This means that the fund realizes a capital gain of $5/share (because it bought at $75/share and sold at $80/share), and thus pays a capital gains tax of, let's say, $1/share (20%). This tax will come out of the fund's year-end distribution to its investors, including YOU.[2] How fair is this to you?

Of course, I think it's not fair at all. Not only did you lose $10/share on ABC's value decline, but in effect you are also paying taxes on capital gains that you personally did not experience and enjoy. Some of the fund's capital gains on ABC stock *might* go to you at the year-end distribution to all shareholders, but note that a $5/share capital gain, net of $1/share expenditure in taxes, does not offset your actual experienced loss of $10/share.

> *According to Morningstar, the average cost of mutual funds' tax inefficiency is between 1% and 1.2% per year.*
> http://news.morningstar.com/articlenet/article.aspx?id=373782

At this point, you've got to be surprised. You might even find my numerical illustration to be so unbelievable that you feel that it cannot be true. Well, I invite you to take my numerical example and to show it to any mutual fund manager and ask how my analysis is flawed. I am pretty sure he or she will respond in one of the following ways: (1) he or she will look dumbfounded; (2) he or she will offer you an explanation that is so confusing that you are not able to understand it, but it's not because you're not smart; it's because the explanation is intentionally convoluted and vague; or (3) he or she will describe ways in which the problem that I am describing can be offset by the many other actions that the fund will take. For example, the fund manager might say that many other fund activities can occur so that the tax flaw that I am describing could be washed out. But, let's be serious. Wouldn't you prefer that the tax flaw that I am describing simply didn't exist in the first place so that offsetting actions don't need to be taken?

Here's more proof that my numerical illustration describing embedded capital gains can mean a lot of money to you. In my numerical example, you actually deserve a tax *credit*. After all, you personally suffered a stock price drop of $10/share. So, if the capital gains tax is 20%, then you would deserve a $2/share tax credit for your loss. But how is the fund going to get this tax credit for you? Think about it. In this example, at the end of the day, it's only you, not the fund, who ends up experiencing an actual value loss when ABC stock dropped in value. You see, for you personally, the relevant "reference price" of ABC stock is $90 per share since this was the value of the stock when you bought the fund. However, your reference price is not used to calculate your gains or losses when the mutual fund sells

ABC stock. What matters is when the fund buys and sells ABC. (In industry-speak, I guess we would say, "The cost basis that is used to calculate capital gains of ABC stock is not when you bought the mutual fund, but it is when the mutual fund bought ABC stock.") So, not only did you lose $10 per share on ABC stock because of its stock price decline since you bought the fund, but you are also deprived of a $2 per share tax credit.

Now, at this point, you might think that maybe I'm a smart guy and thus I am able to make up a clever, contrived numerical example just to help support my argument that mutual funds often suffer from tax inefficiencies. I have two responses to this assertion. First, thank you for the compliment. Second, it is true that my numerical example is just one of maybe a million possible combinations of odd things that can happen with mutual holdings and activities. And there might be some situations and occurrences where oddities can work in your favor. But, let's get serious. Wouldn't it be best to avoid these odd situations altogether? These are your hard-earned savings that we're talking about. Do you want your savings to be subjected to a bunch of odd effects that you hope will all wash out in the end?

And finally, you don't have to take my word for it that mutual funds can suffer from this tax inefficiency. Just do a Google search on the phrase "mutual fund embedded capital gains," and I bet that you'll get a bunch of results. Actually, I'm going to do this right now, hold on . . . yep,

I got tens of thousands of results. And it's a good thing that I did the Google search, as I came across some other nice descriptions of mutual fund tax inefficiencies. Here's one from Morningstar's webpage:

   Investors in conventional mutual funds can get stuck with a tax bill on their mutual fund holdings, even if they've lost money since they've held the fund . . .

[Hey, this is just like my numerical illustration!]

. . . and they also have to pay taxes on all fund distributions, including capital gains, which occur when a fund manager sells an underlying holding for more than its purchase price.

[See, your own personal reference price of the fund's holding is not factored in anywhere!][3]

And here's some useful text from Wikipedia (what did we ever do before Wikipedia?) that explains the tax inefficiency succinctly:

After purchasing mutual fund shares, an investor will have a tax liability for any net capital gains in the mutual fund portfolio, even if the investments the fund sold for a gain were purchased before the investor owned the shares of the fund. This is known as an "unearned capital gain," and has negative effect on the investor's return from his mutual fund investment.[4]

See, I wasn't making any of this up. At this point, you may feel that the tax inefficiency of mutual funds is a sufficient reason for you to stop considering them as a viable investment option. If so, then no need to read more about mutual funds' flaws—you will find what I believe is a better investment alternative in chapter 9: Are SMAs the Solution?

But please feel free to read on. I've got other surprising reasons why mutual funds are a flawed and obsolete way to invest.

Chapter 2 Notes

1.   Wilcox, R.T. (July 30, 2008). The dangers of embedded tax liabilities in mutual funds. Retrieved from https://usthrift.wordpress.com/2008/07/30/the-dangers-of-embedded-tax-liabilities-in-mutual-funds/

2.   Bergstresser, D. (2002). Do after-tax returns affect mutual fund inflows? *Journal of Financial Economics*, 63, 381–414.

3.   Rushkewicz, Reichart K. (2010, February 15). How tax-efficient is your mutual fund? Retrieved from http://news.morningstar.com/articlenet/article.aspx?id=308356

4.   Separately managed account. (n.d.). *Wikipedia*. Retrieved from http://en.wikipedia.org/wiki/Separately_managed_account

3 | Mutual Fund Hidden Costs

As I mentioned in chapter 1, when you and others buy a mutual fund, you are actually paying a mutual fund firm to own stocks for you. You don't own the stocks directly. Because mutual funds have many investors, YOU can suffer! Unbelievable, right? In fact, many people in the industry refer to these costs as "hidden costs" because many investors are not aware of them due to the fact that they are difficult to calculate.[1, 2, 3]

These costs are considered to be hidden because they are undisclosed. But these hidden costs may actually be *larger* than the mutual fund's disclosed costs.[4] That is, mutual funds might be costing you more than double what you think. Can you imagine that? Let's do some simple math. Let's say that you have $100,000 to invest. You buy a mutual fund with 2% in disclosed fees, or roughly $2,000. Let's say that over the course of a year the market goes up by around 8%, so you think you're going to make $8,000 on your investment, from which you paid about $2,000 in disclosed fees. You would have about a $6,000 return. But, because of the undisclosed "hidden" costs, you might end up "paying" an additional $2,000, thereby reducing your total return to $4,000. So, this means that you "paid" about $4,000 (i.e., $2,000 disclosed cost plus $2,000 hidden cost) to get about a $4,000 return. I guess the hidden costs are why some experts consider mutual funds to be a "drag on your retirement."[5]

You might think that these hidden costs are difficult to explain or understand, but really they are not. I will describe these undisclosed costs now. But to help explain them, I want you to first consider the following two situations, which should help you to understand the costs that I will be describing shortly.

Situation A

During a given week, let's say that a bunch of individual investors decide to **invest** a total of $50 million into a $500 million mutual fund. In this scenario, the fund will take the new investors' $50 million and buy more stocks with it, and then it will become a $550 million fund

Situation B

During a given week, let's say that a number of individual investors decide to **divest** $50 million from a $500 million fund. Here, the fund has to sell $50 million worth of stocks to obtain the cash to give to the divesting investors, and then it will become a $450 million fund.

Now, given the above two situations, there are three costs that YOU can personally suffer because of these other investors' investing and divesting in and out of your fund. I will try to explain each cost in turn.

Commissions

When a mutual fund buys additional stocks to accommodate new investors after you invested in the fund, the fund typically has to pay broker commissions, which can eat away at the value of your investment and your returns.[6, 7] Say that you buy a mutual fund today. Then, next month, the mutual fund receives more cash from new investors. The fund then uses this cash to buy more stocks. The fund pays broker commissions for these trades. But here's the surprising part: because you are a part-owner of the fund, this means you are partially paying for these costs too, even though these trades are not being executed on your behalf. That is, the costs of running a mutual fund are shared among all mutual fund owners. Of course, the fund incurs the same commission costs when investors sell their mutual fund shares. In this example, part of these costs comes

15

out of the amount that you originally invested or out of the distributions that are paid out to all of the fund's investors, including YOU, even though it's the other investors who are causing this cost. Let's just imagine the following scenario. Today, you buy a fund and you hold it, but the fund that you own continues to pay extra brokerage commissions due to *others'* trading. How fair is this to you? Not fair at all.

Okay, that was the easiest of the three costs to explain. Now I'll explain two other subtle costs. And, by the way, just because these other costs can be subtle, that doesn't mean that they cannot significantly impact your wealth.

Trading commissions are estimated to cost mutual fund investors on average 0.25% per year.

http://www.cfapubs.org/doi/pdf/10.2469/faj.v69.n1.6

Bid-Ask Spreads

The bid-ask spread, which describes the second cost, is going to annoy you if you already own mutual funds. Later, when I explain why this cost can be particularly large for some mutual funds, it is likely going to annoy you even more. By the way, don't forget that I'm just the messenger. Don't be annoyed with me.

Have you ever tried selling your used car to a

dealership? If you have, then you're likely familiar with this scenario. You initially plan to sell the car yourself and look up the estimated price of your car on the Internet (maybe you'll use Kelly Blue Book). You discover that your used car is worth a decent amount of money, so you become happy and start imagining ways of how you're going to spend this money. Now, let's say you are feeling busy and decide that you do not want to sell your car yourself after all. For the sake of convenience, you decide to take your car to a car dealership. At the dealership, to your shock and dismay, the car dealer offers you quite a low price for your car, much lower than the estimate you saw on the Internet. You argue with the dealer that your car is worth more, but the dealer gives you his or her reasons for offering a low price. For example, one thing that the dealer might say is "I have to make money on this car." (And you know, this is a fair point. The dealer needs to be, and should be, compensated for his or her service because without the dealer you might not be able to find a buyer at all.) Let's say that you accept the dealer's offer. You go home feeling pretty annoyed.

Have you ever tried buying a used car at a car dealership? If you have, then I bet you felt like you got ripped off or fleeced on the price. At the least, you probably felt unsure about the price that you paid.

The stocks that most of us buy are kind of like used cars. We're buying them from other investors, through securities dealers. Like used car dealers, these securities dealers buy stocks at one price (the "bid price") and resell them at a higher price (the "ask price"). So, just like the car dealer, the ask price is always higher than the bid price. This "bid-ask spread" is a way that securities dealers (and used car dealers) make their money on trades. They buy at bid prices that are lower than their resell prices.

How does all of this bid-ask spread stuff affect you, especially after you buy a mutual fund? Would you sell a $20 bill for $19.50 and buy a $20 bill for $20.50? Of course not. You'd be losing $1 on this "spread." But, after you buy a mutual fund, if your mutual fund continues to buy stocks at a higher ask price and sell at lower bid price, that causes the fund (and thus also YOU) to lose money.[8] In industry-speak, many refer to these losses that occur due to bid-ask spreads as "slippage."[9] Remember Situations A and B above? The fund trades to accommodate investing and divesting investors, so you are stuck paying slippage caused by other investors.

Bid-ask spreads are estimated to cost mutual fund investors on average 0.23% per year.

http://www.cfapubs.org/doi/pdf/10.2469/faj.v69.n1.6

This is making you annoyed, right? Well, I hate to say this, but there's more to these "transactions" costs that I will explain.

Let me now explain how something called "adverse selection" can make bid-ask spreads even wider and how mutual funds, in particular, can especially suffer from this adverse selection problem.[10, 11]

Unlike you and me, mutual funds usually don't buy only hundreds or thousands or even tens of thousands of dollars' worth of stocks. Instead, when a mutual fund buys and sells stocks, the transactions are often quite large. They might, and easily can, for example, buy millions of dollars' worth of Google stock.

So, what's the big deal when a mutual fund buys millions of dollars of stock? Let's say a mutual fund wants to purchase 2 million shares of XYZ Biotech stock. The fund goes to a securities dealer to buy them, but the securities dealer may only have 500,000 shares available to sell at his or her best ask price (a "best ask price" is the lowest standby price that a dealer is ready to sell a stock). Since the fund wants to buy an additional 1.5 million shares of XYZ Biotech stock, it then has to pay the dealer a higher price for those shares. Why doesn't the dealer just sell all 2 million shares for the same price? There is something known as "adverse selection." It's an academic term, but the concept is really easy to understand. If you were a stock dealer, and a mutual fund wants to buy tons of XYZ Biotech stocks from you, wouldn't you think that the fund manager might know something that you don't? Maybe XYZ Biotech stock just got a positive result on a clinical trial, but only the fund manager knows this right now. After all, there are probably a lot of smart people who work at mutual funds. So, to help protect yourself from selling a great stock for a bargain, you might only let mutual funds and other investors purchase a specific number of shares at your lowest ask price. If they want more than this specific amount, then they have to pay a higher price for them. This pricing policy can protect the dealer from selling too many shares of a possibly fantastic stock at a bargain.

By the way, this also applies to mutual funds' *selling* stocks. If a mutual fund wants to sell 2 million shares of XYZ Biotech stock, then the fund may not be able to sell them all to a securities dealer at his or her current "bid price." This means that the fund may have to sell off some of those 2 million shares at lower prices.

Okay, the above is a pretty clear illustration of what adverse selection is and how it works. But you're probably still wondering what this all has to do with you. Well, imagine this. You buy a mutual fund today. And then, you hold your shares in that mutual fund. But the fund is still actively buying and selling stocks, especially given the fact that other investors are investing into the fund and divesting from the fund. This means that mutual funds often place very large orders to buy and sell stocks and that a part of their large orders to buy may get filled at very high ask prices and a part of their large orders to sell may be filled at very low bid prices.[12]

In other words, because mutual funds make large orders to buy and sell stock, they may experience large bid-ask spreads. I already told you how these spreads can lose you money. Well, what I'm telling you now is that these spreads can be especially large for mutual funds. (And, by the way, don't make the mistake of thinking that a mutual fund can get a "large quantity discount" or a good price just because it is buying lots of stocks. That'd be pretty funny. I know the price of donuts and the price of wine are cheaper when you buy them by the dozen, but you can't say to a securities dealer, "I'd like to buy a lot of IBM stock, and since I'm buying a lot, can you give me a discount or can you give me a few IBM shares for free?")

So, overall, bid-ask spreads almost certainly lose you money. Therefore, you can actually be losing this money even if the mutual fund is NOT doing any of this buying or selling on your behalf! And, these spreads could be huge because of adverse selection!

Speaking of large buy and sell orders, they not only cause bid-ask spreads to widen, they can also have another adverse effect on you! Read the next section. *Warning: reading farther may annoy you even more.*

Price Impact

This cost is related to the above bid-ask spread and adverse selection costs, but it's also a unique cost in and of itself. Let's say that AAA Small Cap stock is currently priced at $20 per share. Now let's say that you want to buy a million shares of AAA Small Cap. Do you think you can buy them all at $20 per share? Based on what I wrote above, you already know that you probably cannot because of bid-ask spreads and adverse selection. But let's ignore bid-ask spreads and adverse selection for now.

Let me repeat the question—do you think you can buy a million shares of AAA stock for $20 a share? Probably not. You see, when there is a large demand for something, then the price of that something usually goes up. It's not rocket science, it's logical, and it's really that simple. Why are Super Bowl tickets so expensive? It is partly because there is a high demand for those tickets. Large demand can affect stock prices too.[13] If someone buys a million shares of a stock, that stock price will usually rise, simply from the large buy order in and of itself. This effect is called "price impact."

So, how does this price impact cause you to lose money? Imagine the following. You buy a mutual fund, and then you hold it. However, when the mutual fund buys stock, it isn't very likely to be buying a few shares of stock. Instead, it is likely to be buying many thousands or even millions of shares of stock. Right now, let's say your mutual fund owns BBB Mid Cap stock currently worth $80 per share. If the fund decides to buy a million more shares of BBB Mid Cap stock, this large demand by itself may cause BBB Mid Cap's share price to increase. Let's say that it increases to $81/share (some of the increase is coming from adverse selection and some of it is coming from the price impact of the mutual fund's trade).

Now, do you see what's about to happen? Your fund is going to pay $81 for an $80 stock. Do you like paying more than what something is worth? Of course not. Have you ever said to anyone, "I'll pay you $21 for a $20 bill?" Of course you haven't. But that's what your mutual fund will be doing. Remember, BBB stock is currently worth $80 per share. But because of the mutual fund's large buy order, it could cause the stock price to go up and the fund may end up paying, let's say, $81 per share. This extra $1 payment has to come from somewhere. From where? From all of the investors in the fund, including you. This specific cost to mutual fund investors is pretty well-known and is sometimes referred to as a "market impact cost," and it has been suggested that this cost is quite significant.[14]

And, of course, this price impact effect can apply to mutual funds' selling stocks, too. Price impact typically has bad consequences for you. If your mutual fund *sells* a million shares of BBB Mid Cap, the large sale order by itself might cause BBB Mid Cap's stock price to fall, let's say, to $79/share. Remember, BBB Mid Cap shares are really worth $80 each. Do you want your mutual fund to sell BBB Mid Cap shares for less than what they're worth? Have you ever said to anyone, "I'll sell you a $20 bill for $19?" Of course you haven't. But the fund's large sell order, by itself, could drive the stock price down. Your fund now has $79 in cash instead of an $80 stock. And by the way, maybe this $79 per share is just short of the $80 per share that the fund needed to raise, and thus it has to sell more BBB Mid Cap stock at $79/share to cover the difference.

So, price impact typically affects you negatively. The large buying and selling that mutual funds do, in and of themselves, cause stock prices to increase and decrease.[15] Under this example, the fund buys stocks for more than what the stocks are really worth, and the fund sells stocks for less than what they are really worth. As I said before, this is like buying $20 bills for $21 *(some of the extra $1 is coming from the spread, and some of it is coming from the price impact)* and selling $20 bills for $19 *(some of the $1 loss can be due to the spread, and some of it can be due to the price impact).* The takeaway from this discussion is simple: you may be losing money due to a mutual fund's trading even when you hold your shares of a mutual fund.

Now, at this point, I want you to realize the following. If you own your own personal portfolio of stocks, then it is unlikely you will be buying millions of shares of any stock. After all, you are not a large financial institution like a mutual fund with billions of dollars to invest on behalf of thousands or millions of investors. So, if you decide to buy and sell BBB Mid Cap stock, it will probably not affect the stock price at all. That is, you won't experience the adverse effects of price impact because your individual and relatively small trade sizes will not cause stock prices to move. In other words, you won't suffer from market impact costs.

But wait! There's more to the hidden costs caused by price impact.

When a stock's price increases only because one mutual fund buys a lot of that stock, the price increases tend to be temporary.[16] Think about it. In this example, the price change is NOT occurring for any fundamental reason. That is, the stock price is not increasing because the firm discovered a new invention or innovation, discovered oil, or hired a great CEO. Instead, the stock price is increasing because the mutual fund is simply buying lots of stock when new investors buy into the fund. Typically those stock prices will come back down to their fundamental levels.

So, here's a summary of the overall "impact" of price impact, which can consist of two parts. First, the fund submits a large buy order for a stock, causing the stock price to increase, which, in turn, can lead to the fund paying more for the stock than what the stock is really worth. So, for example, the fund pays $81 for an $80 stock. Here, you lose a dollar. But, you might say, "Okay, I get it, the fund spent $81 for an $80 stock, and I realize that stinks, but at least the fund owns what is now an

$81 stock." Okay, get ready for the second part.

After the fund buys the stock, the stock price will typically revert back to its original fundamental value, because, in our example, the fundamental value is the original price. So, the fund could pay $81 for an $80 stock, and after it buys the stock, the stock will eventually go back to $80.

> *Price impact is estimated to cost mutual fund investors on average 0.94% per year.*
>
> http://www.cfapubs.org/doi/pdf/10.2469/faj.v69.n1.6

Playing Devil's Advocate

Before I conclude this chapter, let me offer the following. Whenever anyone makes an argument, he or she should always consider opposite viewpoints. So, I'd like to do that now. As I review this chapter's contents, I think the only issue that a detractor could raise is that bid-ask spreads are not as large as they used to be. This is a fair point. Are you old enough to remember when stock prices were in increments of one-eighth of a dollar? I am. Actually, this wasn't that long ago. Today, stock prices are decimalized, so that the smallest price increment is a cent. So, in the "old days," the smallest bid-ask spread that you could possibly have was one-eighth of a dollar (12.5 cents), but today, the spread can be only a penny. This means that the bid-ask spread cost that I described in section 2 may be minor. So, even though you could continue to suffer costs after you buy a mutual fund, these costs may be small. Does this make you feel better? Wouldn't it be better if you didn't suffer any of this cost at all? And, by the way, when anyone uses the point that "today's spreads are smaller than they used to be," ask him or her about the effect that I describe in section 2, that adverse selection can make spreads wider. The person might also say that the adverse selection effect is also smaller today because we now price stocks in decimals (i.e., in cents). I would actually dispute this point. We all know that spreads can be narrow when there are a lot of buyers and sellers (i.e., when there is a liquid market). But in the scenario that I described in section 2 there is a single large buy (or sell) order submitted by a single mutual fund. In such a scenario, the spread can be large. But okay, okay, I don't want to get into an argument over whether adverse selection costs are big or small. We can all agree that a cost exists, and that's my main point.

By the way, I'm not done. Also ask my detractors about the price impact effects that I described. Are they small today too? They might say so, arguing that markets are more efficient today than they used to be. But at some point, the sum of a bunch of small costs could equal a big cost.

So, overall, I do not think my detractors have much of a case.

> *"We found that funds' annual expenditures on trading costs (hereafter, aggregate trading costs) were comparable in magnitude to the expense ratio (1.44% versus 1.19%, respectively)."*
>
> http://www.cfapubs.org/doi/pdf/10.2469/faj.v69.n1.6

Other Costs

Before I conclude this chapter, there are a few other costs that I should mention. Mutual funds have extra expenses that many other investments do not. Mutual funds usually have to pay for the following[17]:

- Administrator

- Accountant

- Auditor

- Board of Directors

I should imagine the above are not cheap. I guess this is part of the reason for why mutual fund fees are so high.

On to the next chapter.

Chapter 3 Notes

1. Edelen, R., Evans, R., & Kadlec, G. (2013). Shedding light on "invisible" costs: Trading costs and mutual fund performance. *Financial Analysts Journal*, 69(1). doi: 10.2469/faj.v69.n1.6. Retrieved from http://www.cfapubs.org/doi/pdf/10.2469/faj.v69.n1.6

2. Prior, A. (2010, March 1). The hidden costs of mutual funds. *Wall Street Journal*. Retrieved from http://online.wsj.com/articles/SB10001424052748703382904575059690954870722

3. Mahoney, P. G. (2004). Manager-investor conflicts in mutual funds. *Journal of Economic Perspectives*, 18, 161–182.

4. Bernicke, T. A. (2011, April 4). The real cost of owning a mutual fund. Forbes. Retrieved from http://www.forbes.com/2011/04/04/real-cost-mutual-fund-taxes-fees-retirement-bernicke.html

5. Tuchman, M. (2014, February 19). A hidden way mutual funds cost you money. *Forbes*. Retrieved from http://www.forbes.com/sites/mitchelltuchman/2014/02/19/a-hidden-way-mutual-funds-cost-you-money/

6. Prior (2010).

7. Edelen et al. (2013).

8. Prior (2010).

9. One example of the use of the term "slippage" when referring to losses that occur due to bid-ask spreads is here: Wide bid/ask spreads & slippage are costing you $3,840 each year (n.d.). Retrieved from: http://optionalpha.com/show-026-wide-bidask-spreads-slippage-are-costing-you-3840-each-year-17607.html

10. A basic definition of "adverse selection" is here: Adverse selection. (n.d.) *Wikipedia*. Retrieved from http://en.wikipedia.org/wiki /Adverse_selection. The term is often used to explain why insurance companies charge high premiums and limit coverage. Specifically,

because insurance companies are aware that high-risk individuals are the ones that specifically seek insurance, the insurance companies charge high premiums and limit coverage to them.

11. Academic papers that describe how adverse selection affects bid-ask spreads include the following:

    —Heflin, F., & Shaw, K. W. (2005). Trade size and informed trading: Which trades are "big"? *Journal of Financial Research*, 20, 133–163.

    —Affleck-Graves, J., Hegde, S. P., & Miller, R. E. (1994). Trading mechanisms and the components of the bid-ask spread. *Journal of Finance*, 49, 1471–1488.

    —Stoll, H. R. (1978). The pricing of security dealer services: An empirical study of Nasdaq stocks. *Journal of Finance*, 33, 1153–1172.

12. Market makers (finance). (n.d.). Retrieved from http://what-when-how.com/finance/market-makers-finance

13. Edelen et al. (2013, pp. 7–8) describe how "price impact" impairs mutual fund returns. Some academics call it a "price pressure" effect, for example: Ben-Rephael, A., Kandel, S., & Wohl, A. (2011). The price pressure of aggregate mutual fund flows. *Journal of Financial and Quantitative Analysis*, 46, 585–603. An academic paper that broadly describes how large buying and selling causes this price impact effect is Harris, L., & Gurel, E. (1986). Price and volume effects associated with changes in the S&P 500 list: New. *Journal of Finance*, 41, 815–829.

14. Prior (2010).

15. Prior (2010).

16. Ben-Rephael (2011, p. 14).

17. Mutual fund. (n.d.). *Wikipedia*. Retrieved from http://en.wikipedia.org/wiki/Mutual_fund

4 | Mutual Fund Under-Performance

Here's a mystery. Why do mutual funds underperform? This underperformance is notoriously well-known and sometimes even joked about in the popular press,[1,][2] and it is also a subject of much study in academia.[3] Why do these so-called professional money managers underperform? Truly, this is bizarre.

We often hear that picking stocks that will outperform is so hard to do that if you were to throw darts randomly at a list of stocks and create a portfolio consisting of these dartboard stocks, that it would do just as well as stocks picked by so-called experts. This notion is so popular that the *Wall Street Journal* used to feature a "dartboard column" where they pitted so-called expert stock pickers against randomly chosen stocks.[4] The pros beat the dartboard a little bit more than half the time.[5] You would think, therefore, that just based on randomness, mutual funds would be known for pretty much *matching* the market's performance, *on average,* rather than underperforming the market.

> *"On average, active funds underperformed by around 1.6 percentage points a year, a big handicap for clients. There was one year, 1999, when most funds underperformed but the average return was slightly higher than the market. Still, the average return only beat the market 6 times out of 20."*
>
> http://www.economist.com/blogs/buttonwood/2015/02/mutual-fund-investing

Many possible explanations have been put forth for why mutual funds underperform. Here are just five possible causes that I think are the most plausible (and, by the way, I'm ignoring mutual funds' disclosed fees, which is another obvious reason why actively managed mutual funds might not generate the same returns as the market).[6]

First, most mutual funds suffer from undisclosed "hidden" costs, which we covered extensively in chapter 3. The undisclosed "hidden" costs of mutual funds are likely to be one of the primary causes of their underperformance.

2) Second, for mutual fund managers, their fund's performance is typically not directly linked to their compensation. Therefore, for instance, a fund manager may not be paid based upon his or her success in generating gains for investors. A fund manager most often gets compensated from the fees he or she charges for managing the fund, which is typically a percentage of the fund's total assets. In this scenario, a fund manager's compensation will increase when the fund increases in size, and therefore, fund growth becomes one of the manager's primary goals.[7] If the fund manager sees his or her primary goal as fund growth, this is likely different from your goal, which I'm guessing is to get nice returns on your mutual fund investment. This difference in goals is known as the principal-agent problem or agency costs of mutual funds. That is, it's your money, so you're the principal, and you "hire" an agent (the mutual fund manager) to manage your money in the fund, but the two of you could have different goals. There is academic research that indicates that these differing goals contribute to fund underperformance.[8]

Third, there seems to be a lot of turnover of mutual fund managers. For example, good mutual fund managers seem to be going to hedge funds that are willing to offer higher pay. As a result, many mutual funds may have inexperienced managers, and this might explain their underperformance. In fact, academic studies support this contention.[9] This is kind of funny because many investors probably think that the value added of investing in a mutual fund is the fund manager's investing expertise and experience, but you could lose your fund manager and his or her expertise and experience due to turnover, and the replacement manager may have neither. Further, for those funds that did well in the past, investors might buy them, thinking that the fund will continue to do well in the future, BUT because of manager turnover, it's quite possible that the manager responsible for those great past returns is no longer with the fund.

Fourth, did you know that some funds even outsource management? Many people buy mutual funds because they think the mutual fund firm will manage them. What's wrong with outsourcing the management of the fund? Well, according to academic studies, when mutual funds outsource fund management, they underperform.[10]

Finally, mutual funds may be over-diversified by holding "too many" securities.[11] This "over-diversification" may be driving down the fund's ability to obtain good returns. This over-diversification problem of mutual funds is so significant, and really a problem all on its own, that I feel that it deserves its own chapter. So . . .

Chapter 4 Notes

1. Durden, T. (2013, January 5). 88% of hedge funds, 65% of mutual funds underperform market in 2012. Retrieved from http://www.zerohedge.com/news/2013-01-05/88-hedge-funds-65-mutual-funds-underperform-market-2012

2. Freeburn, C. (2012, September 24). 2012 banking survey: Banks go fee happy. Retrieved from http://investorplace.com/2012/09/2012-banking-survey-banks-go-fee-happy/#.U86c2_ldXoQ

3. Fama, E. F., & French, K. R. (2010). Luck versus skill in the cross-section of mutual fund returns. *Journal of Finance*, 65, 1915–1947.

4. Ensign, R. L. (2013, April 14). Darts top readers in final print contest. *Wall Street Journal*. Retrieved from http://online.wsj.com/ news/ articles/10001424127887324 50470457841086400087264.2

5. Investor Home—The Wall Street Journal Dart Board Contest. (n.d.) Retrieved from http://www.investorhome.com/darts.htm

6. See the second point raised in this article: Finger, R. (2013, April 15). Five reasons your mutual fund probably underperforms the market. *Forbes*. Retrieved from http://www.forbes.com/sites/richardfinger/2013/04/15/five-reasons-your-mutual-fund- probably-underperforms-the-market

7. Cohen, R., Polk, C. &, Silli, B. (2010, March 15). Best ideas. SSRN working paper, p. 2.

8. Mahoney (2004, p. 164).

9. Golec, J. H. (1996). The effects of mutual fund managers' characteristics on their portfolio performance, risk and fees. Financial Services Review, 5, 133–147.

10. Chen, J., Hong, H., Jiang, W., & Kubik, J. (2013). Outsourcing mutual fund management: Firm boundaries, incentives, and performance. *Journal of Finance*, 68, 523–558.

11.   Haigney, A. (2012, March 13). The curse of over-diversification. *Business Insider*. Retrieved from http://www.businessinsider. com/the-curse-of-over-diversification-2012-3

5 | Mutual Fund Over-Diversification

Warning—even though this is a pretty important chapter, it is also a really long chapter (it even has a subchapter). So, I'll provide you with the "CliffsNotes" version of the points that I am going to make in this long chapter:

- Portfolio diversification can be great.

- But analysis shows that you can achieve the benefits of portfolio diversification with only around twenty-five to seventy-five stocks.

- Many mutual funds contain hundreds of stocks,

which suggests that some stocks are just fillers, that is, not the fund managers' favorite stocks.

- Mutual funds also may hold hundreds of stocks because of regulations, industry structure, fund manager incentives, and fund company goals. These incentives and goals may not fully align with the goals of mutual fund investors. As a result of the above, mutual funds tend to underperform benchmarks.

A professional basketball team consists of up to thirteen available players with different skillsets.[1] Some players may be good passers, some may be good at defense, some are tall, and some are fast. That is, a basketball team can be thought of as a diversified portfolio. And yet, the thirteenth player on the team rarely plays. This is because basketball coaches often feel that they can get more out of their best players than they can from their thirteenth best player, even though the thirteenth best player may be different from all of the other players.

Let's suppose you're ordering some ice cream, but you don't know which flavor you'll like. Which would you choose: a bowl of ice cream with three different flavors of your choosing or a bowl of ice cream with five hundred different flavors? With the former, there's a good chance you'll like at least one of the flavors. With the latter, well, that's just going to taste weird. But more specifically, you won't be able to taste the best flavors because they'll be diluted.

What's the point of the basketball and ice cream discussions? They are my way of showing you that diversifying too much can sometimes be a bad thing. If the basketball coach was forced to use his thirteenth best player the same amount as his starting five players, then his team will likely lose a lot. If you were forced to mix all the available ice creams, you likely wouldn't even want a free serving. Similarly, portfolio over-diversification can dilute fund performance because the manager is invested in too many securities.

To understand the problem with stock portfolio over-diversification, it is useful to do a quick review of diversification in general. Let me do that now.

Diversification 101

Portfolio diversification, in and of itself, can be a great thing, but only if it follows sound risk/reward principles. For example, if a portfolio is broadly diversified across different asset types, then it will likely improve one's risk/reward tradeoff. But a nice risk/reward tradeoff cannot always be achieved by simply holding many assets, especially if the assets are similar.

Let me illustrate what I mean by starting off with an example. Let's say that you have a portfolio containing only two stocks, ABC stock and XYZ stock, and you own an equal dollar amount of each stock in your portfolio. And let's say there are only two possible future outcomes,

Outcome 1 and Outcome 2, and that each outcome has a 50% chance of occurring. So, given the above simple situation, let's say that there are three possible scenarios:

Scenario 1:

	ABC Stock Returns	XYZ Stock Returns	Portfolio Returns
Outcome 1	16%	10%	13%
Outcome 2	-4%	-2%	-3%
Expected Return	6%	4%	5%

Scenario 2:

	ABC Stock Returns	XYZ Stock Returns	Portfolio Returns
Outcome 1	16%	4%	10%
Outcome 2	-4%	4%	0%
Expected Return	6%	4%	5%

Scenario 3:

	ABC Stock Returns	XYZ Stock Returns	Portfolio Returns
Outcome 1	16%	-2%	7%
Outcome 2	-4%	10%	3%
Expected Return	6%	4%	5%

Now, pay attention. We're going to do a little Finance 101. In Scenario 1, if Outcome 1 occurs, then your portfolio will generate a 13% return, the average of one stock in your portfolio, which got a 16% return, and the other stock, which got a 10% return, [i.e. (16%+10%)/2=13%]. If Outcome 2 occurs, then your portfolio will suffer a 3% loss, since one stock suffered a 4% drop and the other stock suffered a 2% decline [((-4%)+(-2%))/2=-3].

Now, since there is a 50% chance of Outcome 1 occurring and a 50% chance of Outcome 2 occurring, then this means that the *expected* return on your portfolio is 5%, the simple average of a 13% portfolio return (in Outcome 1) and a 3% portfolio loss (in Outcome 2) [(13%+(-3%))/2=5%]. Simple to follow, right?

Scenario 2 is the same as Scenario 1, except XYZ returns are the same 4% in both outcomes.

Scenario 3 is also the same as Scenario 1, except now the two stocks move in opposite directions. That is, when ABC has positive returns, then XYZ has negative returns. And when ABC has negative returns, then XYZ has positive returns.

Now, check this out. The expected portfolio returns of all three scenarios are an *identical* 5%. But which scenario has the safest portfolio? Of course, it's the one in Scenario 3. You expect a 5% portfolio return, but the worst that can happen is that you get a 3% return. Hey, that's not very risky! The standard deviation of this portfolio is only 2%.

Which is the riskiest portfolio? Of course, it's the one in Scenario 1. You again expect a 5% portfolio return, but this time the worst that can happen is that you suffer a 3% loss. Whoa, this is risky. You can lose money in Scenario 1. The standard deviation of this portfolio is 8%.

Why is Scenario 3 safest? It's actually easy to see. It's because the returns of ABC stock and XYZ stock are negatively correlated. That is, when one stock suffers a loss, the other stock enjoys a gain. In fact, in Scenario 3, no matter which outcome occurs, you always have one stock giving you a positive return.

> *Standard deviation is sort of the "average" amount that returns on investment can deviate from their average expected return. It is a commonly used measure of variability, so it can be used as a measure of investment risk.*

Overall, there are a two amazing things about this simple numerical example. First, it shows that you can reduce risk, *without* sacrificing returns. There's a popular saying, "Less risk, less return." Well, in my example, you can reduce risk without sacrificing returns. This is why proper portfolio diversification can be so beneficial to performance. If you had to sacrifice returns to obtain risk reduction, we academics and industry professionals wouldn't be tooting the horn of diversification.

However, you may be one of those people who sees the glass as "half-empty" and contends that Scenario 3 is not good because you will *always* have a stock with negative returns. Here is my response to you: what sacrifice are you making in Scenario 3 since *all* of the portfolios in the above three scenarios are giving you the *same* expected 5% returns? If the portfolio in Scenario 3 gives you the same return as the portfolios in the other scenarios, but with the lowest risk, you're not making any sacrifice at all.

Scenario 1:
You have two risky stocks moving in the same directions

	ABC Stock Returns	XYZ Stock Returns	Portfolio Returns
Outcome 1	16%	10%	13%
Outcome 2	-4%	-2%	-3%
Standard Deviation	10%	6%	8%

Scenario 2:
You have one risky stock and one safe stock

	ABC Stock Returns	XYZ Stock Returns	Portfolio Returns
Outcome 1	16%	4%	10%
Outcome 2	-4%	4%	0%
Standard Deviation	10%	0%	5%

Scenario 3:
You have two risky stocks moving in different directions

	ABC Stock Returns	XYZ Stock Returns	Portfolio Returns
Outcome 1	16%	-2%	7%
Outcome 2	-4%	10%	3%
Standard Deviation	10%	6%	2%

With regard to the second amazing thing about my simple example, let's look at the three scenarios again, and let's look closely at the risks of each stock and also of the portfolios. For your convenience, I've replicated the previous tables, but this time I replaced expected returns with standard deviations, which is a common measure of stock risk. A higher standard deviation indicates riskier stocks.

By focusing on the standard deviations, you can see the second amazing thing about my simple example. The table above shows that it is possible to own two risky stocks (this occurs in Scenario 3) and have a safer portfolio than owning one risky stock and one safe stock (this occurs in Scenario 2)! Look at Scenario 3. Wow, those two stocks are risky. ABC stock has a standard deviation of 10% while XYZ stock has a standard deviation of 6%. I look upon these as pretty large standard deviations, especially relative to each of their individual expected returns. Now look at Scenario 2. Here, ABC stock is as risky as it is in Scenario 3. However, XYZ stock has a standard deviation of 0%, so it has NO risk. But look at the portfolio standard deviations of Scenarios 2 and 3. The standard deviation is lower in Scenario 3, only 2%, even though it contains two risky stocks with large standard deviations. Ta da! Two risky stocks may sometimes be safer than one risky stock and one safe stock. Counter-intuitive, right? But it's true!

Of course, sometimes a portfolio with two risky stocks can combine into a risky portfolio . . . duh. This is what happens in Scenario 1. That portfolio has two positively correlated risky stocks, and that portfolio is the riskiest of the three scenarios. So again, portfolio diversification can be amazing, but only if you know how to do it or have someone who does help you.

For the most part, pioneering economist Harry Markowitz is credited with the above discoveries. He's the one who suggested that we should select stocks that are not strongly positively correlated to one another.[2] And for this discovery, he won the 1990 Nobel Prize in Economics.[3]

So, this is one strategy that I think good money managers should follow. They should try to pick stocks with low or negative correlations with each other to help minimize risk without sacrificing returns. This approach can be achieved by a qualified finance professional who understands these principles. You know how in those exciting car commercials, in which professional drivers push cars to their limits, there is always the caption, "Do not try this at home. These are professional drivers"? Well, I guess I could say the same thing about replicating Scenario 3—"Do not try this at home." I believe that Scenario 3 is a strategy that is best left to professional money managers.

Now let's make a realistic extension to my simple, made-up numerical example. Instead of only two stocks and only two possible outcomes, let's think about stock returns in the real world. In my simple example, I assumed that I knew what ABC stock's and XYZ stock's returns would be in the future under each of the three scenarios. Of course, in real life, we cannot predict stock returns this accurately. So, even when we think stock returns will be negatively correlated or uncorrelated with one another, we could be wrong.

A second important point about the real world is that there will always be some risk that we cannot eliminate. For example, if we discover that a firm's executives have been lying about the firm's earnings, disclosure of this fact may cause the firm's stock to take a nosedive. Or, if a star CEO gets hit by a car and dies, then her firm's stock might free-fall. Obviously, we can never reliably predict these "random" events. Finance professionals normally call the chance of random occurrences "idiosyncratic risk."[4]

Do you think that holding a portfolio of only two stocks is sufficient diversification to cover idiosyncratic risk? I don't. So, the question is, how many more stocks do you need to hold to obtain the benefits of portfolio diversification? I'll show that you don't need to hold hundreds of stocks and why owning too many stocks would be potentially harmful over-diversification.

How Many Stocks Are Needed to Diversify a Portfolio?

How many stocks should you hold in a portfolio? Actually, not that many. Academic research has proposed that the full benefits of diversification can be achieved with as few as ten stocks,[5] but we think that holding between twenty-five and seventy-five stocks per portfolio is a good guide.[6,7] Table 1 shows the expected standard deviation of annual returns of portfolios with different numbers of stocks.[8] As shown in the table, the benefits of diversification increase trivially if one increases his or her holdings from seventy-five stocks up to hundreds of stocks.

Table 1: **Portfolio Diversification**

Number of Stocks	Standard Deviation
1	49.236
2	37.358
4	29.687
6	26.643
0	24.903
10	23.932
12	23.204
14	22.670
16	22.261
18	21.939
20	21.677
25	21.196
30	20.870
35	20.634
40	20.456
45	20.316
50	20.203
75	19.860
100	19.686
200	19.423
300	19.336
400	19.292
450	19.277
500	19.265
600	19.247
700	19.233
800	19.224
900	19.217
1000	19.211
Infinity	19.158

Hmmm, this table is kind of annoying to look at. Let me convert it into a figure. And besides, I like pictures. See Figure 1:

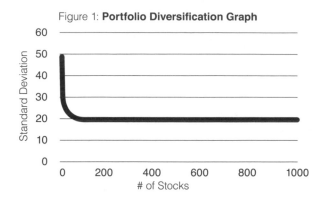

Figure 1: **Portfolio Diversification Graph**

In Figure 1, the number of stocks in the portfolio is on the horizontal axis, and the expected standard deviation of the portfolio is on the vertical axis. As you can see from the figure, as the portfolio contains more stocks, the risk goes down. But do you see how there's almost no difference in risk between holding seventy-five stocks and holding a thousand stocks? Now, let me just show the standard deviation of a portfolio for only up to a hundred stocks. See Figure 2:

Figure 2 is really helpful because we can now see more precisely that the benefits of risk reduction provided by adding more stocks is pretty small after you already have twenty-five stocks. Twenty-five stocks, that's it![9]

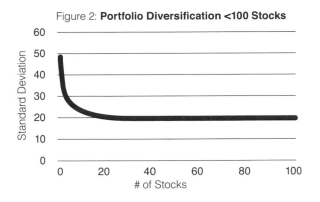

Figure 2: **Portfolio Diversification <100 Stocks**

Now, you probably want to know how these standard deviations were calculated. Because, after all, you may feel like you don't know whom to trust since I've been telling you that you should be skeptical of mutual funds. I have to admit that the math used to derive the standard deviations in these tables and figures is kind of complicated, so let me show you a simple illustration that helps demonstrate that holding hundreds of stocks may be unnecessary.

Why Don't You Need Hundreds of Stocks to Be Diversified?

Now, don't forget my previous numerical portfolio diversification example with Scenarios 1, 2, and 3. I was able to create a really safe portfolio with only two stocks, stocks ABC and XYZ. But that was an overly simplified example. In reality, as I previously mentioned, returns can be hard to predict, especially given idiosyncratic risk.

Now, before we go any farther, let's clarify one thing. Many people in the finance and investments industry like to refer to idiosyncratic risk as the "sh*t happens" risk. On the one hand, I have to admit that this is a good way to describe randomness, but, on the other hand, it suggests that all random occurrences are bad, and, of course, this isn't necessarily the case. Just the other day when I picked up my carryout order from my favorite Vietnamese restaurant, the restaurant was about to close and another customer had not shown up to pick up his order. So, the restaurant just let me have his carryout order for free. That was lucky and random. And not only that, the free food that I got was something that I liked, even though I'm kind of a picky eater. Now that was really lucky and, again, random. And, on my way home, I found a thousand dollar bill! Okay, that last part didn't happen, but if it had, that also would have been a random occurrence. And all of these random occurrences can be considered good outcomes.

Companies can also experience random good luck. For example, a company could accidentally discover a cure for erectile dysfunction (true story, as Pfizer wasn't trying to find a cure for erectile dysfunction when they discovered Viagra),[10] or a company, 3M, could accidentally discover Post-it Notes (another true story).[11]

Now, given that a random occurrence can be either a good thing or a bad thing and given that randomness can imply a fifty-fifty chance that a random outcome will be good or bad, note the following. Let's say you own only two stocks, and something random happens to both firms of those stocks. In this case, there is a 25% chance that *both* firms will experience random bad luck.[12] Yikes, that's risky!

Now let's say that you own 25 stocks. And let's also say that something random happens to all of the firms of those 25 stocks. Here, there is only a 0.0000003% chance that all firms will experience random bad luck. [13] Wow, that is some HUGE risk reduction! When you go from having two stocks to 25 stocks, you go from a large 25% chance that of all of your stocks will experience bad luck to a miniscule 0.0000003% chance that all of your stocks will experience bad luck. How this happens is not hard to understand. When you own 25 stocks, it's simply more likely that you will experience around an equal amount of good luck and bad luck. We have a saying for this phenomenon, "It'll all come out in the wash." For example . . .

Me: Darn, I forgot my wallet. Can you pay for our lunch?

My Friend: Sure. No problem.

Me: I promise that I'll pay you back.

My Friend: Don't worry about it. It'll all come out in the wash.

What my friend is saying is that he and I will go out to eat many times in our lives and even though most of the time neither one of us will forget our wallet, sometimes he may randomly forget his wallet, so I'll have to pay for both of us, and sometimes I may randomly forget my wallet, so he'll have to pay for both of us. Eventually, neither one of us is likely to have paid much more than the other. Of course, this kind of eventual canceling-out can only happen if we go out to eat a bunch of times. The same kind of canceling-out can happen when you own a bunch of stocks, such as twenty-five stocks. Most of the time, random things may not happen. But when random things do occur, it's okay if you own enough stocks such that the bad luck occurrences and good luck occurrences cancel out.

However, despite my claim that significant risk reduction can be achieved with only twenty-five to seventy-five stocks, I cannot think of any mutual fund that only has this many stocks in it. Instead, they often hold hundreds of stocks.[14] To me, this is somewhat perplexing. And given that many mutual funds in fact actually focus on narrow investment styles, such as large cap value, small cap growth, and so on, I would think that most mutual funds would actually hold *fewer* than seventy-five stocks. After all, if your focus is narrow, then it can be easier to be diversified within that narrow focus (e.g., for a large cap fund, they don't need to hold small cap stocks).

But mutual funds, even those focused on a specific investment style, can often hold hundreds of stocks.

Now, let me ask you the following question. Do you think that a mutual fund manager can identify hundreds of great stocks? If so, then what's your definition of "great"? By definition, a great stock has to be one that is better than the majority of other stocks. So, if a mutual fund has hundreds of stocks in it, then it probably contains some great stocks but also some stocks that are merely "fillers." These filler stocks may be the cause of mutual fund underperformance.[15] Without these filler stocks, shouldn't a mutual fund that only contains great stocks do well? If the answer is "yes," then question is, "Why do mutual funds hold so many stocks?" In other words, why do they *over-diversify*? I will outline a few possible reasons next.

Why Do Mutual Funds Over-Diversify?

There are several possible reasons why mutual funds over-diversify. First, mutual fund managers who only hold twenty-five stocks in their funds may feel limited in their ability to charge high fees. After all, investors might wonder why it's so expensive to manage twenty-five stocks. So, fund managers may hold many more stocks to help justify high fees.[16]

Second, there are regulations that prevent mutual fund managers from being heavily concentrated in a few stocks.[17] So, to help make sure they are compliant with regulations, mutual fund managers may hold hundreds of stocks just to make it abundantly clear that they are not heavily concentrated in a few stocks. The Investment Company Institute also recognizes this tendency. From its handbook:

> If a fund elects to be diversified, the Investment Company Act requires that, with respect to at least 75 percent of the portfolio, no more than 5 percent may be invested in the securities of any one issuer and no investment may represent more than 10 percent of the outstanding voting securities of any issuer.[18]

In practice, most funds that elect to be diversified are much more highly diversified than they need to be to meet these two tests.

Third, if a mutual fund does well, then you as an investor are probably happy, but the fund manager doesn't directly benefit much from the outperformance. But if the fund does poorly, then the fund manager might get fired by his or her mutual fund firm.[19] When mutual fund managers consider these two divergent outcomes, they may feel it is better to prevent the underperformance rather than to go for the outperformance. So they buy many, many stocks in effort to prevent underperformance. I wouldn't blame them for behaving this way. I think you and I might behave similarly because we'd want to keep our jobs.

Fourth, mutual fund managers may be overly fixated on driving down risk to improve their Morningstar Ratings.[20] In general, mutual fund managers want to obtain four- and five-star ratings from Morningstar, which is a famous research firm that evaluates and rates mutual funds.[21] If a mutual fund obtains a high rating from Morningstar, then it is likely to attract more money from investors. And don't forget from chapter 4 that mutual fund managers want to manage more money, as this is how they can make more money from management fees.

One of the most important criteria to obtain a four- or five-star rating is to have a high Sharpe Ratio, which is simply a ratio of the fund's excess returns to its risk (I will describe Sharpe Ratios in detail later, and I will also describe the fallacy of Sharpe Ratios). So, to help obtain a high Sharpe Ratio, a fund manager could either try to find stocks with high future returns or try to reduce risk. As you can imagine, the latter is much easier to do than the former. Think about it. If I told you that your life depended on either buying stocks with high future returns or buying stocks to minimize risk, then you would obviously do the latter because all you would need to do is simply buy hundreds of stocks. Guess what? It looks like this is what many mutual fund managers do. However, overemphasis on improving return/risk ratios by driving down risk can lead to over-diversification, which I explained earlier and may be unnecessary.

But, while it may be unnecessary to be over-diversified, is it a bad thing? I'm glad that you asked.

Why Over-Diversification Can Be a Bad Thing

Okay, so we now know that holding hundreds of securities may be unnecessary, so you might be thinking to yourself, "Okay, I get it, being over- diversified may be unnecessary, but so what?" I have a couple of points to make here. The first you probably already see coming. By being too fixated on reducing risk, you may be foregoing nice returns. Later, in chapter 5a, I illustrate that portfolios with high Morningstar Ratings (due to high Sharpe Ratios) could deliver inferior returns.

The second point is somewhat related to the first point, but it is also a unique point in and of itself. When mutual funds add many stocks to their portfolios only to drive down idiosyncratic risk to raise their Sharpe Ratios, this can mean that the positive impact of the few great stocks that the fund owns will get watered down. That is, given that fund managers are supposed to be investment experts, they may know of a handful of great stocks with promising returns, but they may purposely water down those returns by adding lots of "filler" stocks to their portfolios. This over-fixation on Morningstar Ratings and Sharpe Ratios may mean that fund managers are diluting the nice returns being generated by their good stock picks! In fact, this has already been discovered.

Mutual Fund Managers' "Best Ideas" Can Get Watered Down

In a study by professors at Harvard and the London School of Economics, the authors find that fund managers' best stock picks (i.e., their "best ideas") outperformed benchmarks by about 1% to 4% per quarter.[22] How did the researchers know which stocks were the fund managers' favorites? Simple: they identified the stocks in the managers' portfolios with the highest representation. So, if fund managers know how to pick good stocks, then why don't mutual funds outperform benchmarks? The authors conclude that fund managers fill out their portfolios with filler stocks, for reasons similar to those that I just described. By the way, this study was independently verified by a professor at the University of Toronto.[23]

And it's not just academics who know that too many stocks may "spoil the broth." Here's a nice snippet from Investopedia:

Dilution—It's possible to have too much diversification. Because funds have small holdings in so many different companies, high returns from a few investments often don't make much difference on the overall return. Dilution is also the result of a successful fund getting too big. When money pours into funds that have had strong success, the manager often has trouble finding a good investment for all the new money.[24]

A nice thing about the Investopedia quote is that it also describes how over-diversification can be caused by a fund getting too big. This, too, has been supported by academic research. For example, one study states, "We first document that fund returns, both before and after fees and expenses, decline with lagged fund size, even after accounting for various performance benchmarks."[25]

So, size can matter. It seems that funds should not have too many stocks and that they should not be too big. Both can water down returns.

Conclusion

Here are the main takeaways of this chapter:

- Portfolio diversification can be great.

- Academic research shows that you only need twenty-five to seventy-five stocks to achieve essentially the full benefits of stock portfolio diversification.[26]

- But mutual funds still may hold hundreds of stocks because of regulations and the flawed incentives faced by fund managers and fund companies.

- The above seem to cause mutual funds to underperform benchmarks.

The next chapter is sort of like an appendix to chapter 5. It provides an in-depth discussion on why Sharpe Ratios are often a flawed way to evaluate portfolios. You should read it because many investors, including so-called sophisticated institutional investors, rely heavily on Sharpe Ratios to evaluate mutual funds. But I think such a heavy emphasis on Sharpe Ratios is highly misplaced.

Chapter 5 Notes

1. You might think the number of active players on a professional basketball team is twelve (in fact, I did), but according to the latest collective bargaining agreement, the number is now thirteen. Check this out: https://en.wikipedia.org/wiki/ NBA_Collective_Bargaining_Agreement#Roster_size

2. Markowitz, H. M. (1959). *Portfolio selection: Efficient diversification of investments.* New Haven, CT: Cowles Foundation for Research in Economics at Yale University.

3. Nobel Prize in Economics. (n.d.). *Wikipedia.* Retrieved from http://simple.wikipedia.org/wiki/Nobel_Prize_in_Economics

4. Idiosyncratic risk. (n.d.). *Investopedia.* Retrieved from http:// www.investopedia.com/ terms/i/idiosyncraticrisk.asp

5. Evans, J. L., & Archer, S. H. (1968). Diversification and the reduction of dispersion: An empirical analysis. *Journal of Finance, 23,* 761–767.

6. Statman, M. (1987). How many stocks make a diversified portfolio? *Journal of Financial and Quantitative Analysis, 22,* 353–363.

7. Elton, E. J., Gruber, M. J., Brown, S. J., & Goetzmann, W. N. (2010). *Modern portfolio theory and investment analysis.* 8th ed. Hoboken, NJ: Wiley.

8. Statman (1987, pp. 353–363).

9. Elton et al. (2010, pp. 353–363).

10. Jay, E. (2010, January 20). Viagra and other drugs discovered by accident. *BBC News.* Retrieved from http://news.bbc.co.uk/2/hi/health/8466118.stm

11. Editors of Publications International, Ltd. (2007, September 19). 9 things invented or discovered by accident. Retrieved from http://science.howstuffworks.com/innovation/scientific-

experiments/9-things-invented-or-discovered-by-accident.htm

12. The way that I estimated the 25% probability is as follows: $0.50n = 0.25$ when $n = 2$ stocks. This estimation is based on the assumption that the probability of good luck versus bad luck is 50% each and that causes of bad luck and good luck are independently and identically distributed. You know, here's a better way to explain it. It's like flipping a coin twice. There's a 25% chance that I'll get two heads and a 25% chance that I'll get two tails. There's a 50% chance that I'll get one head and one tail because either the first flip can be a head and second flip a tail (25% chance), or the first flip can be a tail and the second flip a head (25% chance).

13. $0.50n = 0.00000009\%$ when $n = 30$ stocks.

14. Cohen et al. (2010).

15. Cohen et al. (2010, p. 2).

16. Cohen et al. (2010).

17. Roet, M. J. (1991). Political elements in the creation of a mutual fund industry. *University of Pennsylvania Law Review*, 139, 1469–1511.

18. Quoted text is from Investment Company Institute. (2014). 2014 investment company fact book. Retrieved from http://www.icifactbook.org/index.html

19. Lippert, R. L. (1996). Agency conflicts, managerial compensation, and firm variance. *Journal of Financial and Strategic Decisions*, 9, 39–47.

20. Bhardwaj, S. (2012, March 5). Mutual fund ratios: Sharpe and Treynor. Retrieved from http://articles.economictimes.indiatimes.com/2012-03-05/news/31124018_1_treynor-ratio-risk-adjusted-sharpe-ratio

21. Cohen et al. (2010).

22. Cohen et al. (2010).

23. Pomorski, L. (2009). Acting on the most valuable

information: "Best idea" trades of mutual fund managers. Working paper, University of Toronto.

24. Quoted text is from Investopedia: Mutual fund. (n.d.). *Investopedia*. Retrieved from http://www. investopedia.com /terms/m/mutualfund.asp

25. Chen, J., Hong, H., Huang, M., & Kubik, J. D. (2004). Does fund size erode mutual fund performance? The role of liquidity and organization. *American Economic Review*, 94, 1276–1302.

26. Elton et al. (2010, pp. 353–363).

5a | The Sharpe Ratio Fallacy

Many investors, along with Morningstar, seem to rely heavily on Sharpe Ratios when evaluating portfolios. So you might want to understand why I think this extreme attention to Sharpe Ratios is ill-advised.[27] If not, then you can skip this chapter, but I think the remaining chapters, especially the last chapter, are really important.

Here is the usual measure of the Sharpe Ratio:

(Portfolio return – risk-free return) / standard deviation of portfolio return.[28]

The numerator is the excess (or extra) return that a portfolio provides beyond the return on a risk-free investment. Usually, we tend to think of Treasury Bills as risk-free investments. The denominator is simply a measure of risk. We tend to think that return volatility is a good way to measure investment risk. That is, you might expect a 15% excess return, but if the returns can vary by a lot, then that's considered risky. The formula is not complicated. Overall, the Sharpe Ratio simply reports the tradeoff between risk and return. But that is all that it is! Nothing more, nothing less. Therefore, the Sharpe Ratio is only reliable and really useful when two portfolios have (1) the same returns but different risk or (2) the same risk but different returns. Let me demonstrate with a simple illustration.

Let's say that Portfolio A and Portfolio B have the same 10% average annual excess return (e.g., 12% portfolio return − 2% risk-free return = 10% excess return) in the past three years but experienced different risks. Let's say Portfolio A's past three-year annual returns had a standard deviation of 7% while Portfolio B's past three-year annual returns had a standard deviation of 8%. So . . .

Portfolio A's Sharpe Ratio = 1.43 (i.e., 10%/7%)

Portfolio B's Sharpe Ratio = 1.25 (i.e., 10%/8%)

Portfolio A has a higher Sharpe Ratio than Portfolio B. And, clearly, Portfolio A is better than Portfolio B. Portfolio A delivers the same excess return as Portfolio B, but with less volatility (i.e., less risk).

Now let's say that Portfolio A and Portfolio B have the same 7% risk but different excess returns (10% vs. 11%). So . . .

Portfolio A's Sharpe Ratio = 1.43 (i.e., 10%/7%)

Portfolio B's Sharpe Ratio = 1.57 (i.e., 11%/7%)

This time Portfolio B has a higher Sharpe Ratio than Portfolio A. And, clearly, Portfolio B is better than Portfolio A. Portfolio B delivers more returns than Portfolio A but with the same risk exposure.

However, in real life, two portfolios are unlikely to have the exact same excess returns or the exact same risk. As such, Sharpe Ratios often cannot tell you which portfolios are obviously better. For example, let's say that Portfolio A has 11% average annual excess returns and 8% risk, while Portfolio B has 10% average annual excess returns and 7% risk. This means . . .

Portfolio A's Sharpe Ratio = 1.38 (i.e., 11%/8%)

Portfolio B's Sharpe Ratio = 1.43 (i.e., 10%/7%)

Here, Portfolio B has a higher Sharpe Ratio than Portfolio A. But can you really tell me that Portfolio B is obviously the better portfolio? For me personally, I'd go for Portfolio A. I'm willing to take on a little extra risk for the extra return.

Here's more proof that Portfolio A above is better than Portfolio B.

Let's pretend we invest $1 million in each portfolio. To make this really easy, let's also pretend, from now on, that the risk-free return is 0% (we can get away with this because the Treasury rates currently are close to 0%[29]). For Portfolio A, at 11% annual returns, after one year you'll have $1.11 million. After the second year, you'll have 11% more for a total of $1.23 million (i.e., $1.11 million times 1.11). After four years, you'll end up with $1.518 million. For Portfolio B, at 10% annual returns, after four years, you'll end up with only $1.464 million. I put these numbers in Table 1.

Table 1:

	Portfolio A	Portfolio B
Today	$1.000 million	$1.000 million
1 year later	$1.110 million	$1.100 million
2 years later	$1.232 million	$1.210 million
3 years later	$1.368 million	$1.331 million
4 years later	$1.518 million	$1.464 million

So, obviously, in this example you'll end up with more money with Portfolio A. This part, of course, you already know. The issue that we need to address is the fact that Portfolio A has more risk. Portfolio A's standard deviation is 8% as opposed to Portfolio B, which has a lower standard deviation of only 7%. To compare both portfolios while considering this difference in risk, here's what I will do. For Portfolio A, in the first and third years, I will use a 19% return, and in the second and fourth years, I will use a 3% return. Why will I do this? Well, when you take the four returns, 19%, 3%, 19%, and 3%, the average is 11%, and the standard deviation is 8%.[30] Don't forget that Portfolio A has a return of 11% and a risk of 8%. For Portfolio B, in the first and third years, I will use a 17% return, and in the second and fourth years, I will use a 3% return. The average of 17%, 3%, 17%, and 3% is 10%, and its standard deviation is 7%. Don't forget that Portfolio B has a return of 10% and a risk of 7%. To see what happens, let's look at the results below in Table 2.

Table 2:

	Portfolio A	Portfolio B
Today	$1.000 million	$1.000 million
1 year later	$1.190 million	$1.170 million
2 years later	$1.226 million	$1.205 million
3 years later	$1.459 million	$1.410 million
4 years later	$1.502 million	$1.452 million

There are two revealing observations from Table 2. First, we see that both portfolios experience lower values after four years when compared to Table 1. That is, in Table 1, Portfolios A and B will be worth $1.518 million and $1.464 million, respectively. In Table 2, Portfolios A and B will only be worth $1.502 million and $1.452 million, respectively. This is not surprising. Volatile returns will bring down the future value of your portfolio, which is one of the adverse effects of volatile returns.

The second revealing observation from Table 2 is really the amazing one—you still end up with more money with Portfolio A, despite its higher risk! Sure, the returns fluctuate more in Portfolio A than in Portfolio B, but do you really care?

At this point, the only thing that I can think of that might still make you think that Portfolio B is better is than Portfolio A is that Portfolio A has a higher probability of having a big downward movement than Portfolio B because, after all, Portfolio A has a higher standard deviation than Portfolio B. Okay, that's a damn good point. But, err . . . this is kind of awkward . . . your point is not valid. Sorry about that. Here, I'll show you. Let's say Portfolio A has a negative return of −2% in year four. And, let's say Portfolio B never experiences a negative return. This is your point, right—that Portfolio A is more likely to experience a big downturn than Portfolio B, given the fact that Portfolio A has a higher standard deviation? So, let's see what happens. And, by the way, to make sure that Portfolio A still maintains a standard deviation of 8% and an average return of 11%, I'll use the following four returns: 13%, 20%, 13%, and −2% (in fact, the standard deviation of these four returns is actually 8.03%, which is larger than 8%, which should, I suppose, help your point even more). For Portfolio B, I will keep its returns the same as in Table 2. The new Portfolio A results are below, in Table 3.

Table 3:

	Portfolio A	Portfolio B
Today	$1.000 million	$1.000 million
1 year later	$1.130 million	$1.170 million
2 years later	$1.356 million	$1.205 million
3 years later	$1.532 million	$1.410 million
4 years later	$1.502 million	$1.452 million

You can see from Table 3 the loss that Portfolio A experiences in year four. It goes from a $1.532 million portfolio to a $1.502 million portfolio. The portfolio loses $30,000. I have to admit—that's a lot of money. But in the end, Portfolio A still gives you more money than Portfolio B, even though Portfolio A experiences a loss while Portfolio B never experiences a loss. The reason why Portfolio A does better is simple—it simply has higher returns.

By the way, an additional nice point that can be made

from Table 3 is that there will be times when a riskier portfolio can lose you money, but, overall, losing some money on a great portfolio will often be worth it. For example, would you rather be given a million dollars and then lose 10% of it, or would you rather be given a hundred dollars and then lose none of it? Obviously, you prefer the former, even though there can be a loss of what you're given. So, you just have to keep these risks in perspective. Here, let me help illustrate with a picture because, after all, a picture is supposedly worth a thousand words.

Let's pretend that there are two funds, Dashed Fund and Dotted Fund. I will graph their pretend performances over a twelve-year period in Figure 1. The fund value is on the vertical axis and the year is on the horizontal axis.

Figure 1:

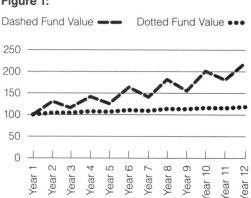

By the way, the data that I used to draw the graph in Figure 1 is provided in Table 4. I want to show you these values because I want to be fully transparent.

Table 4:

	Dashed Fund Value	Dotted Fund Value
Year 1	100	100
Year 2	130	104
Year 3	115	103
Year 4	140	107
Year 5	125	106
Year 6	160	110
Year 7	140	109
Year 8	180	113
Year 9	155	112
Year 10	200	116
Year 11	180	115
Year 12	220	119

Now, I have a simple question: which fund would you rather own? Dashed Fund or Dotted Fund? Take a look at Figure 1. Obviously, Dashed Fund looks better, both (1) at the end of the entire twelve-year period and (2) any time during the twelve-year period. But guess what:

Dashed Fund's Sharpe Ratio = 9.18%/19.26% = 0.48

Dotted Fund's Sharpe Ratio = 1.62%/2.31% = 0.70

Based on the returns of the twelve years and based on the standard deviation of those returns, Dotted Fund has a higher Sharpe Ratio! So, based on Sharpe Ratios, you might mistakenly think Dotted Fund is better. Obviously, in this example, Dashed Fund is better.

Finally, I'd like to end my overall point on a high note. So, here it is. Let's go back to Figure 1, and this time let's say Dotted Fund has a 1.5% annual returns with 0% standard deviation. This is a Sharpe Ratio of positive infinity! To see the new comparison between Dotted Fund and Dashed Fund, look at Figure 2.

Figure 2:

Dashed Fund Value ━━ Dotted Fund Value •••

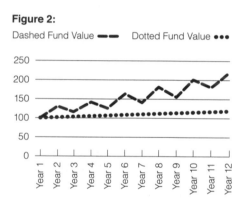

Even though Dotted Fund has an infinitely larger Sharpe Ratio than Dashed Fund, is Dotted Fund the better portfolio in Figure 2? Obviously not. And before you say that there is no such thing as an investment with 0% standard deviation in the real-world, consider that CDs offered by commercial banks are often FDIC insured, which means that the risk is pretty much 0%. As of this writing, the returns on most one-year CDs currently being offered by commercial banks are less than 1% per year.[31] Wow, that's tiny. Really tiny. If you buy a $100,000 CD, you're going to earn under a thousand dollars after an entire year. But because their risk is essentially 0%, this means that these CDs have Sharpe Ratios of positive infinity. Are these CDs super-duper awesome investments? Again, if you believe that high Sharpe Ratios imply better investments, then this means that these CDs are super-duper awesome investments. But obviously these CDs are not super-duper awesome investments.

Need I say more on this topic? Higher Sharpe Ratios, in and of themselves, do not necessarily imply better investments.

Chapter 5a Notes

27. Christian. (2009, March 15). Ah, yes let's dismiss the Sharpe Ratio. Retrieved from http://www.investorgeeks.com/ articles/2009/03/15/ah-yes-lets-dismiss-the-sharpe-ratio

28. Sharpe Ratio. (n.d.). *Investopedia*. Retrieved from http:// www.investopedia.com/terms/s/sharperatio.asp

29. U.S. Department of the Treasury. (n.d.). Daily treasury yield curve rates. Accessed August 31, 2015. Retrieved from http:// www.treasury.gov/resource-center/data-chart-center/ interest-rates/Pages/TextView.aspx?data=yield

30. Technically, we should use geometric means to be more precise, but for the purpose of pedagogy we use the arithmetic average because it's easier to understand and the conclusion is qualitatively similar.

31. I looked up CD rates on bankcd.com on August 31, 2015. The highest available rate on a one-year FDIC-insured CD was 1.29%. Retrieved from http://bankcd.com/cdrates.html

6 | Mutual Fund Non-Transparency

Whew, that last chapter was long and kind of technical. I'll give you a break and make this chapter short.

You may have heard that mutual funds are not transparent. What do I mean by "not transparent"? First, the disclosed costs of mutual funds can be considered not transparent because it can be hard to understand what's behind all those fees and expenses. Second, the hidden costs of mutual funds (discussed in chapter 3) are, of course, not reported, partly because they are hard to estimate. Third, as explained below, most of the time you don't know what's in the mutual fund.

Of the three non-transparencies, which is the most shocking to you? It's hard to pick, right? Because all three are so unbelievable. Mutual funds have confusing costs, hidden costs, and you usually don't know what's in them. Overall, mutual funds are not transparent.

Anyway, that concludes this chapter—well, not really. But I've made my point and so, if you want, you can go to the next chapter, but if you want a little bit more elaboration on the three non-transparencies that I mentioned above, then you can stay in this chapter for a few more minutes.

What's Going On with All Those Costs?

Regarding the first non-transparency, have you ever tried to buy a mutual fund? If you have, then were you confused about what fees you were paying? First, there are shareholder fees, which can consist of front-end loads, back-end loads, purchase fees, redemption fees, exchange fees, and account fees, and then there are also operating expenses (usually expressed as an "expense ratio"), which can include management fees, 12b-1 distribution fees, and administrative costs.[1] Those 12b-1 fees can include distribution and sales fees.[2] Huh?

And many people don't know what front-end and back-end loads even are. Loads are sales charges, usually paid to the broker, and they are deducted from your investment. If the sales charge is upfront, then it's a front-end load. If the sales charge is deferred, then it's a back-end load. These sales charges are different from purchase fees and redemption fees, which are fees paid to the fund, not to the broker.[3] Confusing, right? I think the mutual fund industry gets away with charging all of these fees because investors don't understand all of the different charges.[4]

And finally, another aspect of mutual funds that can make their costs confusing is that there are different classes of mutual fund shares. And these different classes can have different ways of charging fees. Here is a description of those classes and their typical fees.[5]

Class A Shares

Class A shares typically impose a front-end sales load but tend to have lower 12b-1 fees and lower annual expenses than Class B and Class C shares.

Class B Shares

Class B shares typically do not have front-end sales loads, but they may impose a contingent back-end load, a 12b-1 fee, and administrative fees. However, some Class B shares will convert automatically to a class with a lower 12b-1 fee if the investor holds the shares long enough.

Class C Shares

Class C shares might have a 12b-1 fee, administrative fee, and either a front-end or back-end load. But the front-end or back-end load for Class C shares tends to be lower than for Class A or Class B shares, respectively. Unlike Class B shares, Class C shares generally do not convert to another class. Class C shares tend to have higher annual expenses than either Class A or Class B shares.

Class I Shares

Class I shares, otherwise known as "institutional shares," typically have lower fees but require larger investments.

"Hidden" Costs

Regarding the second non-transparency, don't forget that much of the costs to mutual funds can be undisclosed or "hidden." Remember—from chapter 3? I won't elaborate farther on this point since there's an entire chapter already dedicated to it.

You Never Know What's in the Fund

And finally, regarding the third non-transparency, mutual funds are required by regulations to report their holdings only on a quarterly basis[6], and even then, there can be a substantial lag after the quarter-end to publish the report. In other words, the best you can know about the stocks in your fund is a delayed report that is issued only four times per year.[7]

If you directly asked the mutual fund manager, he or she probably won't tell you what's in the fund because he or she's not allowed to tell one investor without telling all investors.[8] A mutual fund manager also might insist that he or she doesn't want to tip off other fund managers to his or her stock picks.[9] To me, this is strange. Isn't it *your* mutual fund? YOU own something, yet you don't even know what's in it. (By the way, if this is okay with you, then I have a sealed cardboard box that I'd like to sell to you for $1,000. Ha-ha, okay, not really, I wouldn't do that to you. And I don't think you would do that to anyone either, right?)

In between its quarterly holdings reports, the mutual fund may buy and sell stocks without you knowing about it. For example, it could buy a stock, watch it sink, and then quickly sell it before the next quarterly holdings report so that you wouldn't know that the fund had made a bad stock pick. Wait, are mutual funds that sneaky? Yes, they can be. Read the next chapter.

Chapter 6 Notes

1. Mutual funds. (n.d.). Retrieved from https://www.sec.gov/investor/pubs/sec-guide-to-mutual-funds.pdf

2. Shurr, S. (2003, August 13). False advertising: The truth about 12b-1 fees. Retrieved from http://www.thestreet.com/story/10107579/1/false-advertising-the-truth-about-12b-1-fees.html

3. Mutual funds. (n.d.). Retrieved from https://www.sec.gov/investor/pubs/sec-guide-to-mutual-funds.pdf

4. Mutual fund. (n.d.). *Investopedia*. Retrieved from http://www.investopedia.com/terms/m/mutualfund.asp

5. The description of mutual fund share classes and their fees come from *Mutual Funds*. (n.d.). Retrieved from https://www.sec.gov/investor/pubs/sec-guide-to-mutual-funds.pdf

6. U.S. Securities and Exchange Commission. (2004, May 10). *Final rule: Shareholder reports and quarterly portfolio disclosure of registered management investment companies*. Retrieved from https://www.sec.gov/rules/final/33-8393.htm

7. Rachleff, A. (2011, January 25). Demand transparency in an opaque mutual fund world. *Advisor Perspectives*, 8(4). Retrieved from http://www.advisorperspectives.com/newsletters11/Demand_Transparency_in_an_Opaque_Mutual_Fund_World.php

8. Dietz, D. (2000, April 26). What's the big secret about mutual fund holdings? Retrieved from http://www.thestreet.com/story/925755/1/whats-the-big-secret-about-mutual-fund-holdings.html

9. Dietz (2000).

7 | Mutual Fund Sneaky Behavior

There are many mutual funds out there, and they are competing to get your money. So, maybe it should come as no surprise that they have engaged in some questionable behavior to get your business. You might be thinking that maybe they're just pushing the limits to get you some extra profit. Unfortunately, it's more than that. Most of the questionable behavior that I am talking about is to trick you. There are so many sneaky things that mutual funds can do that it's hard to decide which of them to describe and where to start. I'll just describe a few sneaky things that they can do, and I'll begin with incubation.

Incubation

Mutual funds will often use their own money to start new funds before they make them available to investors. This practice is called "incubation."[1] In theory, this sounds like a great idea. You know, test something out before making it available to the public. This is what pharmaceutical drug companies do. They test drugs before they sell them. In fact, we want drug companies to do this. However, here's the sad thing. These mutual fund companies can use incubation to trick you. Let me explain how.

Let's say, hypothetically, that two funds are newly created, where each fund contains randomly chosen stocks. Based on randomness, we could figure that there is a 25% chance that both funds underperform the market (this is like saying there is a 25% chance we get two tails on two coin flips), a 25% chance that both funds outperform the market, and a 50% chance that only one fund outperforms the market (this is like saying that on two coin flips, there's a 25% chance you get heads then tails, and a 25% chance that you get tails then heads, so there's a 50% chance of getting one head on two coin flips). Did you notice something? There is a 75% chance that at least one out of two funds will *randomly* outperform the market! That is, there is a 50% chance that one fund will outperform plus a 25% chance that both funds will outperform. In fact, flip a coin two times right now. There's a 75% chance that you'll get heads at least once. Now, at this point, you might be thinking, "So what?" Here's the so what.

A mutual fund manager could start two funds in incubation, knowing that the odds are great that at least one fund will *randomly* end up being an outperformer. When a fund randomly outperforms, the fund manager could then make this fund available to investors and publicly show a "history" of outperformance. As an investor, you might think that the mutual fund manager is great at picking stocks when in fact the "historical" outperformance was actually random. And, by the way, those funds that do not outperform in incubation are typically not made available to the public, so investors likely never know that they even existed.[2] So, the truth is that the fund manager has not demonstrated any special stock-picking skills and is just selling funds that randomly did well during incubation.

Sometimes, an incubated fund that is newly made available to investors might even boast of four consecutive quarters of outperformance. This performance seems impressive, right? But there is actually a 6.25% chance (this is 1 out of 16) that a fund can randomly outperform for four consecutive quarters.[3] So, by creating 16 funds in incubation, there is a good chance that one of them will *randomly* outperform for four consecutive quarters.

Maybe you think that I'm being cynical. After all, it is entirely possible that incubation is truly a good way to "test" a fund before making it publicly available. Indeed, this is probably how mutual funds pitch this practice.[4] But if this were truly the case, then these so-called "tested" funds should continue to outperform after investors buy them, right? Well, I'm sorry to say that it has already been shown funds which outperformed during incubation did not continue to outperform after incubation, indicating that incubated returns were truly random and not indicative of superior stock selection skills of the fund managers.[5]

Incubation sounds inappropriate and deceptive, right? Well, this deceptive practice is so well-known among finance academics that we are told to adjust for these contrived incubation returns whenever we analyze and study mutual fund performance.[6] Specifically, we're advised to eliminate them from studies so as not to contaminate the "real" returns data. For example, in a white paper by two professors at New York University, they state the following:

> There are problems with returns data that a researcher must be aware of. First is the problem of backfill bias most often associated with incubator funds. . . . This causes an upward bias in mutual fund return data. . . . This bias can be controlled for in two ways. First, when a fund goes public it gets a ticker. Eliminating all data before the ticker creation eliminates the bias. Second, eliminating the first three years of history for all funds also eliminates the bias.[7]

In other words, incubator funds' historical returns are so meaningless that they should be ignored.

Feel tricked, right? Here are additional ways that mutual funds try to trick you.

Leaning for the Tape

Recall that mutual fund returns and holdings are usually made available on a quarterly basis. To help prepare for those quarterly reports, mutual funds might try to make things appear rosier than they really are.

Remember "price impact" from earlier in the book? This is where stock prices can increase simply because of some large purchase orders for the stock but for no fundamental reason. Well, if I'm a mutual fund manager and I anticipate that my mutual fund's performance for the upcoming quarter is not going to look great, you know what I could do? I could buy a lot more shares of stocks that my fund already owns to inflate those stock prices. Yep, this is already being done.[8, 9] This is called "leaning for the tape." This is what sprinters do in a race. Ever watch a one hundred-meter race? The racers lean their heads forward at the finish line. This practice is fine for them because the finish line is the end of the short race. But for mutual funds and for most investors, the quarters are not the end. You want to remain in the game. And don't forget that this price increase from "price impact" has been shown to be only temporary. But the costs (commissions, bid-ask spreads, and the artificially inflated cost paid for the stock) can be a drag on total returns.[10]

> *We present evidence that fund managers inflate quarter-end portfolio prices with last-minute purchases of stocks already held. The magnitude of price inflation ranges from 0.5 percent per year for large-cap funds to well over 2 percent for small-cap funds.*
>
> from[9] Carhart, M. M., Kaniel, R., Musto, D. K., & Reed, A. V. (2002). Leaning for the tape: Evidence of gaming behavior in equity mutual funds. Journal of Finance, 57, 661–693.

Window Dressing

Window dressing is the following. Let's say that a fund holds the stock of Bad Company but not the stock of Good Company. During the quarter, let's say that Bad stock does really poorly and Good stock does really great (just based on the stock names alone, you could have predicted this). Now, given this situation, the fund manager probably feels pretty ashamed of himself, and he probably doesn't want anyone to find out about his poor stock selection. But the quarterly reporting is coming up! What can he do? Quick, get rid of Bad stock and buy Good stock! This could hide the bad stock selection. The investors of the fund may never find out. In fact, to the investors, the manager may even look smart. They might think that the manager held Good stock all along and never held Bad stock. Yep, window dressing happens.[11] And it's done to trick us.

> *"We show that window dressing is associated with managers who are less skilled and perform poorly. Further, we find that window dressing is value destroying and is associated, on average, with lower future performance."*
>
> from[8] Agarwal, V., Gay, G. D., & Ling, L. (2013, July 26). Window dressing in mutual funds. SSRN working paper.

Don't think that this trick is harmless or achieves the worthy objective of owning Good Stock at a good time. Trading for the purpose of window dressing entails the real costs of commissions, bid-ask spread, and price pressure that can reduce your returns. Plus, just because Good stock earned a high return last quarter does not mean that it will earn a high return this quarter. If stock picking were that easy, don't you think fund managers would be outperforming their benchmarks?

Remember, window dressing is done to fool you, and it does so at a cost to you.

Not Tricks But Just Some Other Inappropriate Things That Some Mutual Funds Do

You likely are getting the point—mutual funds can be sneaky, so I will just quickly describe a few other inappropriate things that mutual funds do.

> *"We observe that funds that increase risk experience significantly worse subsequent abnormal returns than funds with stable risk levels . . . For example, funds that increase risk the most (in Portfolio 5) exhibit an abnormal return of -22 basis points per month."*
>
> from[12] Huang, J., Sialm, C., & Zhang, H. (2011). Risk shifting and mutual fund performance. Review of Financial Studies, 24, 2575–2616.

Excessive Risk-Taking Near the Quarter-End

As a quarter comes to a close, your mutual fund's returns might be comparable to market returns. As an investor, this is probably just fine with you. But for the mutual fund manager, this is nothing to brag about. In fact, she may even feel like she is not doing her job well. So, the manager might take a bunch of excessive risks near the quarter-end, to see if she can get lucky and boost the fund's returns a bit.[12] This excessive risk-taking usually won't pay off. For the fund manager, if the excessive risk-taking doesn't pay off, then this may be no big deal, as she had nothing to brag about to begin with and she still has nothing to brag about. But the manager's excessive risk-taking might have caused your fund's returns to fall below market returns!

> *Consistent with the reduction of agency problems from greater monitoring, retail funds with an institutional twin outperform other retail funds by 1.5% per year.*
>
> from[13] Evans, R. B., & Fahlenbrach, R. (2012). Institutional investors and mutual fund governance: Evidence from retail–institutional fund twins. Review of Financial Studies, 25, 3530–3571

Favoritism Toward Institutional Clients

When institutions invest in mutual funds, they might actually be getting their money's worth. They usually pay lower fees, and the mutual fund manager will work hard to achieve outperformance for institutional clients.[13] Not surprising. Maybe you'd do the same thing if you were a mutual fund manager. You know, you want to impress the big clients. You want them to be happy. They're the big and sophisticated investors, after all.

But if the mutual fund that you are investing in does not have institutional clients, then the fund manager may not be working so hard, or he may be neglecting your fund while he focuses on other funds with institutional clients.

Using Your Money to Prop Up Their Investment Banking Business

When a mutual fund is affiliated with an investment bank, the fund manager may buy some of the IPOs that the investment bank underwrote if other investors didn't buy up the entire offering. Yep, this happens.[14] I can just picture this:

Investment Banker: I need a drink.

Mutual Fund Manager: Why, what's up?

Investment Banker: The IPO that I underwrote is not getting bought up. I guess I was wrong about bringing that firm public or maybe the offer price was too high. I don't know. I'm scared that I'm going to get fired.

Mutual Fund Manager: Don't worry. I'll use some of my fund's money to buy the remaining shares you have left over.

Investment Banker: Really? You'd do that for me?

Mutual Fund Manager: Not for you, but for the firm. We work at the same firm, you idiot.

Investment Banker: That's awesome. Now I'm in the mood for a celebration drink. Let's go. I'm buying!

As you'd expect, shares that were not easily sold to the public during the IPO tend to underperform after the IPO. Mutual fund owners end up holding the bag of losers.

> *"The average annualized risk-adjusted returns of the portfolio of affiliated funds are 1.08%–1.68% lower than the portfolio of unaffiliated funds. . . . Our results suggest that fund investors are taking a backseat to investment banking profits. This finding is consistent with the idea that investment banks are propping up their underwriting and advisory services, which have lucrative fees (explicit or implicit), at the expense of their fund management business, which is less lucrative."*
>
> from[14] Hao, Q., & Yan, X. (2012). The performance of investment bank-affiliated mutual funds: Conflicts of interest or informational advantage? Journal of Financial and Quantitative Analysis, 47, 537–565.

Conclusion

Mutual funds can be sneaky in ways that can trick you and cost you money.

Chapter 7 Notes

1. Evans, R. B. (2010). Mutual fund incubation. *Journal of Finance*, 66, 1581–1611.

2. Evans (2010).

3. There's a 50% chance that you will get heads on a coin flip. You get this probability; it's just $0.5n = 50\%$ when n = number of coin flips = 1. The probability that you will get heads four times on four coin flips is $0.5^4 = 6.25\%$.

4. I want to cite examples of this, but I don't want to single out any specific mutual fund and make my compliance officer nervous. I'll let you google it. By the way, many mutual funds often describe incubated funds as "limited distribution" funds (see www.investopedia.com/terms/i/incubatedfund.asp), so use this term when googling: *incubated fund*. (n.d.). *Investopedia*. Retrieved from http://www.investopedia.com/ terms/i/incubatedfund.asp

5. Evans (2010).

6. Elton, E. J., & Gruber, M. J. (2011). Mutual funds. Working paper, New York University. Retrieved from http://pages.stern.nyu.edu/~eelton/Mutual% 20Funds4-13-11.pdf

7. Elton and Gruber (2010).

8. Agarwal, V., Gay, G. D., & Ling, L. (2013, July 26). Window dressing in mutual funds. SSRN working paper.

9. Carhart, M. M., Kaniel, R., Musto, D. K., & Reed, A. V. (2002). Leaning for the tape: Evidence of gaming behavior in equity mutual funds. *Journal of Finance*, 57, 661–693.

10. Ultimate guide to retirement. (n.d.). CNN. Retrieved from http://money.cnn.com/retirement/guide/investing_mutualfunds.moneymag/index14.htm

11. Ro, S. (2012, September 26). The truth about "window dressing":
     How some portfolio managers try to dupe their clients at the
     end of every quarter. *Business Insider*. Retrieved from http://
     www.businessinsider.com/yes-window-dressing-occurs-but-
     the-window-dressers-are-taking-a-huge-risk-2012-9

12. Huang, J., Sialm, C., & Zhang, H. (2011). Risk shifting and mutual
     fund performance. *Review of Financial Studies*, 24, 2575–2616.

13. Evans, R. B., & Fahlenbrach, R. (2012). Institutional investors
     and mutual fund governance: Evidence from retail–institutional
     fund twins. *Review of Financial Studies*, 25, 3530–3571.

14. Hao, Q., & Yan, X. (2012). The performance of investment
     bank-affiliated mutual funds: Conflicts of interest
     or informational advantage? Journal of *Financial
     and Quantitative Analysis*, 47, 537–565.

8 | Are ETFs the Solution?

A lot of investors have been buying exchange traded funds (ETFs) lately,[1] and I mean, a lot of people—and they are buying a lot of them! Some of the popularity of ETFs is likely due to investors being fed up with mutual funds.[2] Are ETFs the solution? In my opinion, ETFs are pretty okay. Let's take a close look at them. But first, a definition.

What Are ETFs?

An ETF is a security that typically replicates an index by purchasing many of the same stocks and/or bonds that are in the index. For example, there is the SPDR ETF, which is supposed to replicate the movements of the S&P 500 Index. When the S&P 500 goes up and down, the SPDR ETF is supposed to go up and down with it. Therefore, ETFs can behave like broadly diversified portfolios of securities. Further, they are easy to buy and sell at pretty much any time during the trading day.

And, ETFs can be pretty cheap. That's because most of them are not actively managed.[3] After all, ETFs are simply intended to mimic something that already exists. Because ETFs can be so cheap, they are often thought to be a solution to expensive mutual funds. But, in my opinion, just because something is cheap doesn't mean you should buy it. After all, if I were willing to sell you my toenails for only ten cents, would you buy them?

Let's take a careful look at ETFs. First, the good news.

ETFs: The Good News

ETFs Don't Suffer That Much from Hidden Costs

Recall from an earlier chapter that mutual funds can impose a rather large hidden cost on you. This occurs because you are a commingled investor when you buy a mutual fund. ETFs can also suffer from these hidden costs, as ETF managers must sometimes make trades to accommodate other investors.[4] But from my experience and based on my research, ETFs don't suffer as much from hidden costs as mutual funds do. There isn't any evidence that would suggest otherwise, at least none that I am aware of. So, good news—ETFs don't suffer much from hidden costs.

ETFs May Not Engage in Sneaky Behavior

ETF managers may not be engaging in sneaky behavior. To be honest, I can't believe I'm considering this good news. It reminds me of when I got into trouble when I was a kid. If my parents questioned me about some bad grades or for not doing my chores, I'd retort back, "Give me a break, at least I'm not a drug-addicted serial killer!" I really thought I was making a good point.

So, I think it's kind of sad that not being sneaky represents good news. But, yeah, part of the good news of ETFs is that they are not sneaky like mutual funds.

✗ ETFs Don't Suffer Much from the Embedded Capital Gains Problem

Recall from an earlier chapter that the cost basis of a mutual fund's securities (used for calculating taxes) is not determined by when you purchased the fund, but instead it depends on when the fund purchased the securities. ETFs can also suffer from some of this tax inefficiency because if the composition of the index that the ETF aims to replicate changes, then the ETF may have to trade and realize capital gains.[5] That is, like a mutual fund, the cost basis used for those capital gains is determined by when the ETF purchased the security, not when you purchased the ETF.

But in my experience, and again, this is based on my research, ETFs' embedded gains are smaller and realized less frequently than mutual funds'.[6] So this is good news.

And now the bad news about ETFs.

ETFs: The Bad News

With ETFs, Investors Cannot Tax-Loss Harvest on Individual Securities

When the value of your stocks goes down, you can either hold onto them or sell them. There can be an advantage to doing the latter. When you sell stocks at a loss, you reduce your aggregate capital gains and can reduce your taxable income (up to a limit). This known as tax-loss harvesting. However, investors in mutual funds and ETFs cannot tax-loss harvest on individual securities because mutual funds and ETFs are bundled investments. For example, if ABC stock in a mutual fund or in an ETF suffers a huge loss, you are not able to strip off stock ABC from the fund or ETF to realize your loss on ABC stock. Of course, if you directly owned a portfolio of securities (say, like in a separately managed account, which we discuss in the next chapter) and it included ABC stock, then you would be able to sell just ABC to take advantage of the tax savings.

> *Tax lot harvesting can be important. "By rigorously realizing losses, the median portfolio would add about 27% compared to a pure buy and hold strategy in typical market conditions. Even after liquidation, net of all deferred taxes, this advantage is still an impressive 14%."*
>
> http://www.iijournals.com/doi/abs/10.3905/jwm.2001.320390

ETFs Rarely, and Are Not Meant to, Outperform

As we discussed in an earlier chapter, mutual funds are known for their underperformance.

Disappointing performance is probably why many investors are switching from mutual funds to ETFs. However, keep in mind that ETFs are usually explicitly linked to a benchmarking index. This means ETFs are unlikely to outperform, simply by design. For example, an ETF based on the S&P 500 is not trying to outperform the S&P 500. Oddly enough, however, there is some evidence that ETFs can even underperform their benchmarks.[7] That's weird. But, nevertheless, the main point here is that ETFs are not typically designed to be outperformers.

ETFs May Sometimes Deviate from Their Underlying Value!

This is also weird, but ETFs can deviate from their underlying value.[8] For example, let's say that an ETF holds only two bonds, and it purchased each for $100. This means that the ETF should be valued at $200. This $200 can be referred to as the ETF's net asset value or NAV. Over time, let's say that one of these bonds goes to a $101 valuation and the other bond goes to $103 valuation. That is, a potential investor could buy these two bonds for a total of $204. But it's entirely possible that the ETF holding these two bonds could be priced at $201. That guy who was thinking about buying the two bonds might think buying the ETF is a bargain. Meanwhile, if you already own this ETF, you're probably scratching your head wondering why it's not worth $204. Again, this is weird. But it can happen. On average, ETFs deviate from their NAV by 2.6%.[9]

With ETFs, Investors Cannot Exclude Stocks for Moral or Ethical Reasons

Some people feel so committed to their morals and values that they wish to invest in a way that is consistent with those beliefs. For example, maybe someone who is strongly opposed to drinking and driving does not want to own stock in firms that sell alcohol. Or, maybe someone who is against underage smoking does not want to own stock in firms that sell cigarettes. People who wish to invest according to their values and conscience cannot request the exclusion of specific holdings when buying mutual funds or ETFs. This is because mutual funds and ETFs are bundled investments. Of course, if you directly owned securities, like in a separately managed account, then you would be able to achieve portfolio customization. We discuss separately managed accounts in the next chapter.

Conclusion

ETFs are pretty okay. Not inspired? Read the next chapter.

Chapter 8 Notes

1. Oyedele, A. (2015, April 13). The explosion of ETFs has been unstoppable. *Business Insider*. Retrieved from www. businessinsider.com/etf-total-net-asset-growth-2015-4

2. Chamberlain, M. (2013, July 18). What's the difference? Mutual Funds and exchange traded funds explained. *Forbes*. Retrieved from http://www.forbes.com/sites/feeonlyplanner/2013/07/18/whats-the-difference-mutual-funds-and-exchange-traded-funds-explained/

3. Pareto, C. (2008, March 16). Mutual fund or ETF: Which is right for you? *Investopedia*. Retrieved from http://www.investopedia.com/articles/exchangetradedfunds/08/etf-mutual-fund-difference.asp

4. Henderson, B. J., & Buetow, G.W. (2014). Are flows costly to ETF investors? *Journal of Portfolio Management* 40, 100–112.

5. Justice, P., & Lee, S. (2012, January). ETFs under the microscope: Tax efficiency survey. Retrieved from http://corporate.morningstar.com/US/PR/TaxEfficiencyPaper.pdf

6. Justice, P., & Lee, S. (2012, January).

7. Anderson, T.M. (August 2010). What can go wrong with ETFs. *Kiplinger*. Retrieved from http://www.kiplinger.com/article/investing/T022-C000-S002-what-can-go-wrong-with-etfs.html

8. Pettajisto, A. (2013, September 20). Inefficiencies in the trading of exchange-traded funds, NYU white paper. Retrieved from http://papers.ssrn.com/sol3/papers.cfm?abstract_id=2000336

9. Pettajisto, A. (2013, September 20).

9 | Are SMAs the Solution?

Are separately managed accounts (SMAs) the solution? (Hint: Yes) What if you could hire your very own money manager and have her pick and buy stocks, just for you? This way, you can directly and literally own the stocks while benefiting from professional money management and portfolio diversification, all without having to bear the hidden costs of other commingled investors. These kinds of accounts are often referred to as separately managed accounts (SMAs). SMAs sound pretty slick, right? Perhaps, not surprisingly, this is how wealthy individual investors, university endowments, and many large institutions invest.[1, 2]

Let's review the benefits of SMAs and also their potential problems.

SMAs: Benefits

When owning securities directly in your own SMA, you will neither be affected by the tax inefficiency caused by embedded capital gains, nor will you be affected by the hidden costs caused by commingled investors, and you'll always know what you own, which is unlike owning mutual funds. We discussed the embedded capital gains problem, the hidden costs of commingled investors, and the opaqueness of mutual funds in earlier chapters.

In fact, SMAs can even outperform relative to their benchmarks. Because SMAs are professionally managed and do not suffer from hidden costs, it is possible for them to beat benchmarks.[3] For example, an article in the *Wall Street Journal* reports that SMAs beat mutual funds during the 2008 financial crisis.[4] The same article also cites a Morningstar study that found that SMAs had routinely outperformed mutual funds prior to 2008.

SMAs: Potential Problems

But there are a few potential problems with SMAs. First, the fees can be unpredictable. Some SMA providers have complicated ways of charging their clients, and they can also have a variety of different fees.

Second, an SMA manager may not be an expert in the many different strategies or asset categories. Maybe she is good at picking value stocks but is not an expert at picking growth stocks. Maybe she is good at picking US securities but not knowledgeable about picking emerging markets securities. Maybe she is an expert on traditional investments, such as stocks and bonds, but not knowledgeable about alternative investments, such as commodities and real estate. And finally, maybe she believes in active portfolio management and does not believe in passive portfolio management. In other words, by having an SMA that is overseen by a single manager, you can be undiversified and over-reliant on one person's expertise, which may be narrow or broad.

Third, you may not be wealthy enough to have access to your very own money manager or to an SMA. Many SMA managers require high minimum account values (e.g., one or two million dollars) to invest with them.[5]

Aw shucks. While the benefits of SMAs sound awesome, the hurdles of SMA investing sound pretty insurmountable, don't they?

I've got good news for you. With today's technology, in the twenty-first century, investors can now access all of the advantages of SMAs without suffering from any of their potential problems. That technology is usually made available on what is known as a turnkey asset management platform (TAMP). However, not all TAMPs are the same. I will describe what you should look for in a TAMP. In fact, I will give you a handy checklist. But first, a definition.

What Is a TAMP?

A TAMP is a technology platform that can provide numerous investment vehicles and manage many investment accounts.[6] Because TAMPs employ automated processes using modern technology, they can also do the trading and maintain account administration at high efficiency and low costs. (Maybe this is confusing and hard to imagine. If so, don't feel bad. I work at a TAMP, yet my parents still don't know what I do.)

The important thing that you need to know is that TAMPs allow your financial advisor to focus on you, your risk tolerance, and your financial goals, and not on doing things like picking stocks and bonds, and performing account administration, billing, and reporting. The TAMPs can do this administrative work, but, more importantly, they can make high-quality money managers available. This is why TAMPs have been growing tremendously in popularity.[7]

How TAMPs Can Help Investors

Predictable Fees

TAMPs can have simple and understandable fees. They have the incentive to provide this because they could be offering many different SMAs and the services of many different SMA managers on their platform. With all of these different offerings, the last thing that a TAMP probably wants to do is to make the fees complicated. We all like having choices but not at the expense of it being confusing when paying for them. TAMPs usually understand this. This is one of the reasons for their existence— to make investing in SMAs easy.

UMA Structure

Wouldn't it be great if we could outdo rich people and have a bunch of different specialized managers each focused on his or her specialty, where one manager might specialize in picking large cap stocks, another might specialize in selecting value stocks, another might be an active manager, another might be knowledgeable about investing in commodities or real estate, while yet another might be an expert on foreign stocks?[8] Or better yet, wouldn't it be awesome if we could have access to several money managers that specialize in large cap stocks and have the option of choosing the one that we think is the best at it? And wouldn't it be great if we could have access to several tactical money managers and have the option of choosing the one that we think is best? And so forth. Actually, all of this is possible with today's technology! Such accounts, in which one can own multiple investment vehicles and money managers in a single account, are known as unified managed accounts (UMAs).[9]

Of course, you don't need to make the tough decisions of which money managers or investment strategies to choose. Your financial advisor can do this for you. An advisor, along with her or his client, could sit down and create a unified managed account (UMA) that includes the stock selections of many money managers. Maybe the investor will be advised to go with Manager Bob's selection of growth stocks, go with Manager Sue's selection of value stocks, go with Manager Jill's selection of Asian stocks, and go with Manager Jack's tactical skills. Isn't this great? Your advisor can help you decide which of many money managers you should hire, and the TAMP can provide the technology that makes all of this possible.

Low Minimum Accounts

While SMA managers may require high minimums, it's possible for you to own SMAs with low minimums through a TAMP. How is this possible? It's possible through automation available with today's technology. With automated trading, billing, and reporting, the operating and administrative costs can be kept low. For a single SMA manager to enable all of this automation, the cost could be huge. But a TAMP can enjoy low costs per account due to its scale.

Also, most TAMPs pay lower fees to their money managers. After all, those money managers aren't doing any of the trading and administrating. These cost savings can be passed along to financial advisors so that they can pass along the savings to their clients.

TAMP Checklist

Are you ready to consider investing in an SMA or UMA? Then look for a TAMP. A good one. As mentioned earlier, there are many TAMPs, and they can vary with regard to what they can and do offer. When you make an appointment with a financial advisor that uses a TAMP, we suggest you bring along the following handy checklist, to make sure you are getting the best service for a low cost. I like to call this . . .

The Ten TAMP Commandments

1. **TAMP shalt have a low minimum investment.**
   What is the minimum investment per account? If the amount is more than what you can invest, then disqualify this TAMP.

2. **TAMP shalt have many money managers available per account.**
   How many different managers can you have in a single account? There are so many different ways to invest, so if you cannot get at least ten managers, then we consider this a fail.

3. **TAMP shalt perform rigorous due diligence on all its money managers.**
   Does the TAMP perform rigorous due diligence on its money managers, or does it let just anyone manage money on its platform? I think your advisor should be spending time listening to you and helping you. So, advisors should be freed from having to screen out bad money managers. If the TAMP's money manager due diligence team does not consist of either PhDs or CFAs, then they may not be capable of screening out bad money managers.

4. **TAMP shalt charge reasonable fees.**
   What is the total cost of using the TAMP, including

the platform fee, possible custodial fees, possible account minimum fees, and bundled product costs (for example, mutual fund, ETF, or close-end fund costs)? If the total cost is more than 1.25%, then I feel that's too much.

5. **TAMP shalt make hundreds of stocks available for direct ownership.**
Can the TAMP provide you with direct ownership of more than a few dozen individual equities? Believe it or not, some TAMPs may only provide direct ownership of a dozen or so equities, just so they can claim they are providing SMAs. But a real SMA provides direct ownership of many equities so that your advisor can have the ability to create a directly owned, diversified portfolio that matches your unique needs and goals.

6. **TAMP shalt not primarily offer mutual funds.**
Is the TAMP only providing you with a way to own a bunch of mutual funds? If you want to be invested in SMAs or UMAs, then avoid this TAMP.

7. **TAMP shalt offer only a few carefully selected mutual funds, if any.**
If the TAMP does offer mutual funds, then does it do so for a good reason? There are a few valid reasons for offering mutual funds, such as accessing strategies that cannot typically be executed in an

SMA. Examples are any strategies that involve futures for commodity exposure or options for risk management. But if the TAMP is offering mutual funds whose strategies can be executed through an ETF or SMA, then I think this is a bad sign.

8. **TAMP shalt be run only by highly trustworthy executives.**

Are the members of the TAMP's executive and investment team people you can trust with your life savings? If they don't seem to be caring, intelligent, and experienced, then you should avoid this TAMP.

9. **TAMP shalt provide 24/7 online access.**

Can the TAMP provide you with online access so that you can view all of your current holdings (updated within twenty-four hours)? If not, then don't use that TAMP. There are TAMPs that can provide this level of transparency.

10. **TAMP shalt provide excellent customer service.**

Is the TAMP's customer service team responsive and helpful? If not, don't you deserve better from the people with whom you are trusting your life savings?

Thanks for reading.

Sometimes, as you're about to finish a really good book, you feel sad that it's about to end. Feeling that now?

Anyway, I wish you all the best as you search for and identify the investment solution that you feel most comfortable with. I realize this is an important life decision. After all, we're talking about how to secure your finances for your retirement and legacy. At least you've already done the first part, which is to educate yourself.

Take care and best wishes on reaching and achieving your financial dreams.

Chapter 9 Notes

1. Singh, M. How to invest like an endowment. (n.d.). *Investopedia.* Retrieved from http://www.investopedia.com/articles/financial-theory/09/ivy-league-endowments-money-management.asp

2. McWhinney, J.E. (n.d.). Separately managed accounts: A boon for all. *Investopedia.* Retrieved from http://www.investopedia.com/articles/05/021405.asp

3. McWhinney, J.E. (n.d.).

4. Salisbury, I. (2009, March 12). SMAs beat funds in 2008. *Wall Street Journal.* Retrieved from http://www.wsj.com/articles/SB123679669243098151

5. Mucciolo, C., (2008, January 1). SMAs on the rise. Wikipedia. Retrieved from https://en.wikipedia.org/wiki/Separately_managed_account

6. Turnkey Asset Management Program (TAMP). (n.d.). *Investopedia.* Retrieved from http://www.investopedia.com/terms/t/turnkey-asset-management-program-tamp.asp

7. Turnkey Asset Management Program (TAMP). (n.d.).

8. By the way, if you recall from chapter 5, I mentioned that you only need twenty-five to seventy-five securities within a single portfolio to obtain sufficiently the benefits of diversification. But if you own ten portfolios, then this may mean that you will own hundreds of securities. In my opinion, this is okay, because each of the ten different money managers will hold what they think are the best securities, so you shouldn't suffer from dilution.

9. Unified Management Account—UMA. (n.d.). *Investopedia.* Retrieved from http://www.investopedia.com/terms/u/uma.asp

About the Authors

Dr. Kenneth A. Kim has been a finance professor for twenty years. He has taught at sixteen different universities, including the State University of New York at Buffalo, Georgetown University, and the University of Michigan. He has spent his entire academic career exposing inefficiencies in financial markets and industry through his research (his many academic papers appear in prestigious academic journals, such as the *Journal of Finance, Journal of Business, Journal of Financial Markets,* and *Journal of Financial Intermediation)* and through his teaching (one of his teaching awards was given to him by the governor of Wisconsin and another by the chancellor of the State University of New York system). His desire and dedication to protect and help individual investors led to an appointment as Senior Financial Economist for the US Securities and Exchange Commission in Washington, DC, during the late 1990s. Dr. Kim has been quoted or his research has been cited in numerous print and online media, including the *Wall Street Journal, BusinessWeek, NewsWeek, New York Times, Washington Post, Boston Globe,* MSNBC.com, TheStreet.com, Kiplingers.com, Fidelity.com, CNBC, MSN News, CBS Radio, and National Public Radio. Dr. Kim is now Chief Financial Strategist at EQIS Capital Management, Inc.

Dr. William R. Nelson is a former member of the Chicago Board of Trade and a former professor in the finance and managerial economics department at the State University of New York at Buffalo. When Dr. Nelson was an academic scholar, his primary research (which was published in prestigious journals such as the *American Economic Review, Journal of Economic Behavior and Organization*, and *Public Choice*) focused on how fairness and fair play affect decision-making, choices, and outcomes, and on how to mitigate corrupt behavior. These research interests were spawned from his life-long passion for fairness and fair outcomes, which is why he was particularly keen on coauthoring a book that exposes mutual fund flaws. Dr. Nelson is currently the Chief Investment Officer at EQIS Capital Management, Inc.

Index